ROADS TAKEN

CONTEMPORARY
VERMONT POETRY

ROADS TAKEN

CONTEMPORARY
VERMONT
POETRY

Edited by
SYDNEY LEA *and* CHARD DeNIORD
Former and current Vermont State Poets Laureate

Introduction by
DAN CHIASSON

GREEN WRITERS PRESS *Brattleboro, Vermont*

Printed in the United States

10 9 8 7 6 5 4 3 2

Green Writers Press is a Vermont-based publisher whose mission is to spread
a message of hope and renewal through the words and images we publish.
Throughout we will adhere to our commitment to preserving and protecting
the natural resources of the earth. To that end, a percentage of our proceeds
will be donated to environmental activist groups, The Ruth Stone Foundation,
Frost Place, and The Southern Poverty Law Foundation. Green Writers Press
gratefully acknowledges support from individual donors, friends, and readers
to help support the environment and our publishing initiative.

Giving Voice to Writers & Artists Who Will Make the World a Better Place
Green Writers Press | Brattleboro, Vermont
www.greenwriterspress.com

ISBN: 978-0-9982604-7-1

PRINTED ON PAPER WITH PULP THAT COMES FROM FSC (FOREST STEWARDSHIP COUNCIL)-CERTIFIED, MANAGED
FORESTS THAT GUARANTEE RESPONSIBLE ENVIRONMENTAL, SOCIAL, AND ECONOMIC PRACTICES BY LIGHTNING
SOURCE. ALL WOOD-PRODUCT COMPONENTS USED IN BLACK & WHITE OR STANDARD COLOR PAPERBACK BOOKS,
UTILIZING EITHER CREAM OR WHITE BOOKBLOCK PAPER, THAT ARE MANUFACTURED IN THE LAVERGNE,
TENNESSEE, PRODUCTION CENTER ARE SUSTAINABLE FORESTRY INITIATIVE® (SFI®) CERTIFIED SOURCING.

Contents

Introduction

Of course Robert Frost is the poet everyone associates with my home state of Vermont, yet the poem I often recall as I'm driving north from Boston to Burlington was written by a Connecticut poet (and Frost's sometime rival) Wallace Stevens:

> We live in a constellation
> Of patches and of pitches.
> Not in a single world,
> In things said well in music,
> On the piano, and in speech,
> As in a page of poetry—
> Thinkers wi thout final thoughts
> In an always incipient cosmos,
> The way, when we climb a mountain,
> Vermont throws itself together.
>
> "July Mountain"

I remember reading these lines in *Opus Posthumous* when I was fifteen or so, sitting in the back of the long gone Little Professor Bookstore on Church Street in Burlington: what a thrill it was just to see the name of my state in Stevens's dense crewelwork of language and thinking. It proved to me, somehow, that Vermont existed, and therefore that I existed: the identification was, and is, total.

The "mountain" I imagined was Camel's Hump, with its 360-degree vistas across the Champlain Valley and the Green Mountains. You can substitute your own mountain, which is Stevens's point: our individual imaginations collaborate, silently and in isolation, on the creation of a common reality, something Stevens calls by various names—but here, to my infinite delight, he calls "Vermont." For its part, Vermont depends upon us, depends on our individual audits of its birds and flowers and habits and moods—though it still seems surprised to be seen in this way, hurriedly "[throwing] itself together" like the host of a party whose guests have arrived at the door just a little early.

Roads Taken is itself a "constellation/of patches and pitches." It is proof to me that Vermont will always require the imagination of its citizens to exist. The same could be said, of course, of Texas or California or New York City, places the idea of which has to be tended and maintained by its inhabitants: and yet. Many people move to Vermont because of the idea of it, an idea that has proven remarkably durable over time: as these poems suggest, the idea of Vermont is not always easy to keep in mind, so powerfully do the daily necessities of living there, of surviving there, assert themselves.

This is where Frost comes in: Frost's poems are the great rural instruction manual for our neck of the woods. His influence is everywhere in the poems collected here, which so often take "nature" not as an idyllic refuge but as a site of careful, strenuous, and repeated steps or actions. "The wearing away,/The changing of means" conjured in Ruth Stone's "Speculation" acts, in these poems, as a perpetual call to verbal attention and acknowledgment.

Vermont wants to be written about. Then again, perhaps it does not. The flipside of the state's bounty of significant places, its dramatic changes of season, its customs often unchanged for generations, its beautiful openness to new people and ideas, is a grating skepticism in the air, almost a distrust of language when it exceeds or falsifies the occasion. Louise Glück's "Burning Leaves," a poem that sounds nothing like Frost, is Frost by other means: its description of "the fire" from a leaf pile that "burns up into the clear sky" before threatening to consume everything around it owes something to Frost's "The Need of Being Versed in Country

Things." Often all that can be said of things is what cannot or should not be said: the "last sparks…still resisting, unfinished" represent *something*, and yet "no one knows/whether they represent life or death." Vermont tempts poets to epiphany; then, by staying silent, or cold, or flinty, or dark, it ironizes their praise.

The Vermonters in this book come from and live all over. There is no birth requirement and, luckily for me, no residency requirement. There *is* something like a love requirement. When I cross over the Connecticut river from New Hampshire on I-89, headed home, I am momentarily consoled. I dislike New Hampshire passionately, always have; this is a common feeling among Vermonters. Frost's great poem "New Hampshire" says what can be said for that state, and at considerable length. But it ends very simply: "At present," Frost says, "I am living in Vermont." At present I'm not, but it makes the state even more vivid in my mind.

Dan Chiasson
Wellesley, Massachusetts

Editors' Note

WITH ITS MYSTICAL LANDSCAPE and fiercely self-reliant citizenry, Vermont has inspired poets from its earliest days. This anthology of contemporary Vermont poets represents a wide range of accomplished voices—both young and old, both renowned and relatively unestablished. Their poems offer news, in Ezra Pound's words, that stays news, and they do so in a wide variety of forms and subjects.

While there is no such thing as a particular brand of Vermont poetry, the poems in this volume claim Vermont as their place of origin, bearing witness to the remarkably rich and ongoing legacy of the state's poetic tradition.

The editors regret any omissions of poets who meet our criteria of having published at least one book with a non-vanity press and lived at least five years in Vermont. In addition to these two requirements, the editors also reserve the freedom to exercise their aesthetic judgement in choosing poems that, in their estimation, reflect memorable language and an accomplished sense of craft that does justice to Vermont's strong poetic legacy. We will continue to add deserving poets to this anthology in ensuing editions.

Chard deNiord and Sydney Lea

ROADS TAKEN

CONTEMPORARY
VERMONT POETRY

Paige Ackerson-Kiely

Misery Trail

I spied eleven lank deer in one evening
feeding on different lots.

I thought a lot of those whose kindness like a string on a balloon
held me aloft over numerous grasses
but never a grass unforgettable.

And never in the river the same water over a rock.
To be lonely like your own hand. To be so
goddamn lonely with just a little information.

I spied the telephone ringing the distance
between one stalk of corn and another.
At certain times of day a field can blind you.

So I walked, uncharacteristically slow.
You couldn't know how slow I walked.

Paige Ackerson-Kiely

THE LAST THING YOU SEE

It's not the last thing you see
pulling out of the driveway—

weeds urging the gravel to recede.
A growing over of dimming light.

Goodbye nestled-in spoon.
The tray's infnite holding. Goodbye

what was lifted to the mouth—a pasture
beyond. Ruminants milling the green blades.

It's not the thing you wanted
a piece of: the way it would feel

in a different life. A hand on the small of the back
urging you forward. The way it would feel.

Later, neighbor judgment.
See you, apron accusing.

The ones you love incompletely
the ones you love and suffer—
sheets kicked to the bed's sloped edge.

The way it would look—
can you tell me how it looks?

Where it was last seen? Can you
tell me what color the skin and the eyes?

It's not the last thing you see
pulling out of the driveway.

It looks like I wished I had loved
more. The moon was enough

of a dress. It ran through the woods
is how it felt.

Goodbye cupboard rife. Put
the dog out. The sound of a train

in the distance never really motivated
anything, unless you count the grass—

unless you count the grass lying down at its side.

What is that number precisely? Can you
count it on your hands?

It's not the last thing you see
pulling out of the driveway.

The stars multiplied in the rearview
mirror. The stars that could be dead

flicked over the sky. They were inviting,
like clear ponds where cattle gather.

I was so thirsty, I had to turn around.

Joan Aleshire

PATCH HOLLOW

Snowshoeing the slope—he ahead,
me faltering after, the deer-like dog
following delicately in our tracks—
we were stopped by what lay in the hollow
below us: the village of cellar holes
and lanes lost to snow, where once
houses, barns, a church, store, mill
had been: ruins a hundred years old.

The story of what happened there
changed from teller to teller—
arson, adultery, incest, murder:
surely some form of betrayal.
Nothing that touched us then,
in the cabin snug against the ridge,
fire tonguing the last black log
in the chaste iron stove, turning
our bare skin rose. His hot haste
seemed like love, bucking against me
on the scratchy blanket he brought
for such times on the bare board bunk.

I didn't wonder how he knew so well
every secluded shelter on the trail.
I thought urgency was a sure sign
of love, didn't know a life can turn
on the sound of high heels a man
likes on a hardwood floor more
than his wife's soft slippers;
didn't imagine all the ways
men and women can hurt one
another, or how a town can empty all at once: fear
following the loaded wagons out
in the rush to new good places,
where betrayal hasn't been invented.

Joan Aleshire

FORK AND THE FIELD BEYOND

Broken in two, the summer-kitchen half
rotting into the ground, the tenant house
the farmer would sell for a sum unimaginable
now seemed right for us. I'd found it
years before, driving the back roads
to soothe the child in long afternoons,
and coming to a Y-shaped fork
with a deep green field beyond,
stopped, thinking I'd entered
a secret world, and took the right-
in-every-way branch east,
through a shallow valley
with a house looking over it,
shaded by maples but neglected,
its once-white paint grey
and peeling, its windows
giving no sign of life. Did it
speak to me then of anything
but loss? I didn't know how
it was built to catch the morning
and evening light, the brook
sound and birdsong. How it
would ask to be mended,
and I would agree: able to fix
this one broken thing.

Julia Alvarez

How I Learned to Sweep

My mother never taught me sweeping . . .
One afternoon she found me watching
TV. She eyed the dusty floor
boldly, and put a broom before
me, and said she'd like to be able
to eat her dinner off that table,
and nodded at my feet, then left.
I knew right off what she expected
and went at it. I stepped and swept;
the pt. blared the news; I kept
my mind on what I had to do,
until in minutes, I was through.
Her floor was immaculate
as a just-washed dinner plate.
I waited for her to return
and turned to watch the president,
live from the White House, talk of war:
in the Far East our soldiers were
landing in their helicopters
into jungles their propellers
swept like weeds seen underwater
while perplexing shots were fired
from those beautiful green gardens
into which these dragonflies
filled with little men descended.
I got up and swept again
as they fell out of the sky.
I swept all the harder when
I watched a dozen of them die . . .
as if their dust fell through the screen
upon the floor I had just cleaned.
She came back and turned the dial;
the screen went dark. *That's beautiful,*
she said, and ran her clean hand through

my hair, and on, over the window-
sill, coffee table, rocker, desk,
and held it up—I held my breath—
That's beautiful, she said, impressed,
she hadn't found a speck of death.

Julia Alvarez

HOMECOMING

When my cousin Carmen married, the guards
at her father's *finca* took the guests' bracelets
and wedding rings and put them in an armored truck
for safekeeping, while wealthy, dark-skinned men,
their plump, white women and spoiled children
bathed in a river whose bottom had been cleaned
for the occasion. She was Tío's only daughter,
and he wanted to show her husband's family,
a bewildered group of sunburnt Minnesotans
that she was valued. He sat me at their table
to show off my English, and when he danced with me,
fondling my shoulder blades beneath my bridesmaid's gown
as if they were breasts, he found me skinny
but pretty at seventeen, and clever.
Come back from that cold place Vermont, he said,
all this is yours! Over his shoulder
a dozen workmen hauled in blocks of ice
to keep the champagne lukewarm and stole
glances at the wedding cake, a dollhouse duplicate
of the family *rancho,* the shutters marzipan,
the cobbles almonds. A maiden aunt housekept,
touching up whipped cream roses with a syringe
of egg whites, rescuing the groom when the heat
melted his chocolate shoes into the frosting.
On too much rum Tío led me across the dance floor,
dusted with talcum for easy gliding, a smell
of babies underfoot. He twirled me often,
excited by my pleas of dizziness, teasing me
that my merengue had lost its Caribbean.
Above us, Chinese lanterns strung between posts
came on and one snapped off and rose
into a purple postcard sky.
A grandmother cried: *The children all grow up too fast.*
The Minnesotans finally broke loose and danced a Charleston

and were pronounced good gringos with latino hearts.
The little sister, freckled with a week of beach,
her hair as blonde as movie stars, was asked
by maids if they could touch her hair or skin,
and she backed off, until it was explained to her,
they meant no harm. *This is all yours,*
Tío whispered, pressing himself into my dress.
The workmen costumed in their work clothes danced
a workman's jig. The maids went by with trays
of wedding bells and matchbooks monogrammed
with Dick's and Carmen's names. It would be years
before I took the courses that would change my mind
in schools paid for by sugar in the fields around us,
years before I could begin to comprehend
how one does not see the maids, when they pass by
with trays of deviled eggs arranged in daisy wheels.
—It was too late, or early, to be wise—
The sun was coming up beyond the amber waves
of cane, the roosters crowed, the band struck up
Las Mañanitas, a morning serenade. I had a vision
that I blamed on the champagne:
the fields around us were burning. At last
a yawning bride and groom got up and cut
the wedding cake, but everyone was full
of drink and eggs, roast pig, and rice and beans.
Except the maids and workmen,
sitting on stoops behind the sugar house,
ate with their fingers from their open palms
windows, shutters, walls, pillars, doors,
made from the cane they had cut in the fields.

Ben Belitt

An Orange in Mérida

The orange-peelers of Mérida, in the wrought-
iron midday, come with mechanical skewers
and live oranges, to straddle the paths
on caissons of bicycle wheels
and work in the dark of the plaza, like jewelers' cloths.
The orange is ceremonious. Its sleep
is Egyptian. Its golden umbilicus
waits in pyramidal light, swath over swath, outwitting
the Caesars. It cannot be ravaged by knives,
but clasps its mortality in, like the skin of an asp.
The bandstand glitters like bone, in laurel
and spittle. Behind their triangular
catafalques, the orange-peelers move through the thirst
of the world with Rameses' bounty
caulked into the hive of the peel
while ratchets and wheels spin a blazing
cosmology on their little machines. Under
skewers and handles, the orange's skin
is pierced, the orange, in chain-mail and papyrus,
unwinds the graveclothes of Pharaoh
in a helix of ribbon, unflawed, from the navel's
knot to the rind and the pulp underneath, like a butterfly's
chrysalis. And sleeper by sleeper, the living turn with their thirst
to each other, the orange's pith is broken
in a blind effervescence that perfumes the palate and burns
to the tooth's bite.
          And the dead reawaken.

Ben Belitt

A Stand of Pine

The hemlock stick keeps its christmas
of mid-summer;
fox-brush and fish-tails of fir,
the demoniac bead of the juniper,
building like the weathers of Norway, like the cone and its hackle,
in formal explosions, matted starling feathers,
whose green is not strange to us;
we have wrecked
with this whale and his bill-hook before. The bough
sets a luminous spinnaker
on the sleeping bitumens,
and tacks through the glosses and gums, like a prow.
Beneath—all a summer's disaster:
the conifer breathing through gill-slits,
a pin-wheel of star fish.
                    The spars
of the hemlock sway upward, where
deep in the resin and sea tackle,
the wrack of leviathan stirs.

Partridge Boswell

HUSBANDRY

In the milk-eye of a dying ewe, unfathomable sky.
Crouched in the mudshit straw you cradle her neck
while the young vet eases a syringe under her shoulder
and cries—an unconditional friend for life.

Her embrace recedes past men, pausing
at the woods' far edge. The river shadows
a train's bent moan threading the valley below.
Come spring you'll find her bleached

bones scattered like signs by coyotes
in the black pasture, your first lesson in
the futility of burial. You were new to this too,
learning from what the earth was preordained

and what would grow or fade with neglect—
from damp leaves under the outcrop, defiant tines
of horse tails—or else the hard art of noticing without
grieving: the paddock superseded by burdock

and thistle, rats that scurried from
sweet feed bins at the barn door's roar
to hide in old bales, molasses warm on their breath.
If a mud-matted ruminant has a soul,

how not a man? How did you watch a single
hawk carry away an entire flock of cochins
and imagine you wouldn't be devastated
and revived by the soulful and soulless alike,

saints and scum hanging thick as webs
of haydust from rafters? Tossing and
stacking the loft, load after load in hundred
degree heat, sweat drenched skin plastered

with dried grains and motes of clover
and timothy, then sitting on porch steps
at dusk while kids build and defend castles
of hay, amnesty of burnt arms and necks –

nothing more needing to be lifted beyond
the G major resonance of muscle at rest.
The land lingers suspended in benediction.
The homeless come home with the same dream

they lit out with slung over their shoulder,
scuffed and worn but unchanged
as the eyes of an old friend you assumed
you'd never live to see again.

Between the garden, flock and field
of rocks, what was it you were farming exactly?
Everything else the runoff takes with it come spring,
leaching down to the lees of a manure-fed

cattail pond, where rumor has it the pope
once swam naked as the sun when he was
the schoolmate of neighbors from the old country.
Before he was the pope, before he was anyone.

Partridge Boswell

WONDER

> *There was not even any sound, because of the sand.*
> —Antoine de Saint-Exupéry

the night before the day you stared god in the eye
and god blinked you became the clock we watched
your hours condensed to a holiness of breath deep
in cavernous sleep…or so we assume until you hear
his playing from another room and cock your head
and your own mother goes to ask him to *come in and*
play for your mother I think she likes it and he comes
and sits beside your bed and strums and sings
a Natalie Merchant song he learned your oldest son
who graduates from high school next year while your
youngest little prince dreams in another room he
has all the stars laughing only for him the rhythm
of blood a perpetual song in his chest as your own
rises and falls a leaky raft at sea and you drift far from
everything you'll miss in their lives far from anything
resembling pity or regret eyes closed resigned to never
sighting land again you listen with the faintest smile
on your lips to this strange wondrous music which
seems to be flowing from somewhere deep inside
of you as the shy boy you always liked but never
spoke to approaches and asks you for this dance

Cora Brooks

Keeping

Made out of not much more
than dust and a slip,
We woke to give our breath
to the wind
as it wound around the oaks and pines
to toss the crows up over the village.
We woke the sleepers to watch our breath.
We made a bowl to hold an ocean,
to hold us, to hold the petals, the pages
of our stories, the poems, the chorus
we have become.

Cora Brooks

SOMEONE ASKS YOU

Someone asks you how you are and
you wonder if they notice the slab
of sorrows you've been given to
balance on your head   you

wonder if you should lie about
it if you should say anything
at all   Appearing in public
you could try to be clever and
poetic   you could say

it is a piece of the shore
a shoulder of the sea
once leaned against

or you could say it is one
of the sections of one of the walls
out of the narrow side of winter

you could say you are just
trying it on for size   that you
have it on trial   that you only
have to wear it when it's
raining—the rest of the time
you wear it for fun   that
despite its bulk it does not
distract you from your purpose
that you feel most exhilarated
most honored to be under its
weight while treading water

the truth is   it is an honor

T. Alan Broughton

GREAT BLUE HERON

I drive past him each day in the swamp where he stands
on one leg, hunched as if dreaming of his own form
the surface reflects. Often I nearly forget to turn left,
buy fish and wine, be home in time to cook and chill.
Today the bird stays with me, as if I am moving through
the heron's dream to share his sky or water—places
he will rise into on slow flapping wings or where
his long bill darts to catch unwary frogs. I've seen
his slate blue feathers lift him as dangling legs
fold back, I've seen him fly through the dying sun
and out again, entering night, entering my own sleep.
I only know this bird by a name we've wrapped him in,
and when I stand on my porch, fish in the broiler,
wine glass sweating against my palm, glint of sailboats
tacking home on dusky water, I try to imagine him
slowly descending to his nest, wise as he was
or ever will be, filling each moment with that moment's
act or silence, and the evening folds itself around me.

T. Alan Broughton

Song for Sampson

What did we do for Sampson our cat?
For years we opened cans for him,
we spread out feast after feast
of golden-fleshed salmon, fine bits
of chicken in thick broth, and he ate
both morning and night. Each day
after he scratched his litter box
we emptied whatever he dropped.
Our laps spread like grassy plains,
and he alone was the pride, sunshine
flowing around the slats of the house
that was his cage, spreading over him
like honey, and his fur grew warm.
At night we gave him whatever place
on our bed was without the kicking feet
of our dreams, creatures he could not see
or smell. Often he lay on the rise and fall
of our breasts, the tide of breathing
and slow slap of heart as we rowed
toward morning. We took from him
all propagation and its will, left him
uncertain why faint odors of a passing female
made him stretch and sniff as if he sensed
his own life embalmed in air, a pharaoh's soul.
And this is why he pissed on our shoes—
not out of anger but to help us carry him
with us wherever we walked in the wide
world he could not enter, spreading musk
of Sampson over the surface of earth,
until he became immortal as the darkness
we eased him into, leaving us blessed.

Megan Buchanan

A New and Fervent Domesticity Has Seized Me

okay, I can understand
the boiling pots of strawberries for jam,
these herbs in the window, gray and green,
my daughter's knees like apples
scrubbed with almond soap,
stacks of white cotton diapers
and
my reverence for clotheslines
has been around for years

but this
ironing
of tea towels
in the dark at half-past one?
scrubbing out the fridge (thumb-
nail detail) two weeks in a row?
I can out-sweep Cinderella,
I'm suspicious of the dishwasher
and I have mastered
all the dagger and caterpillared attachments
of the vacuum

this is inexcusable,
this pressing of creases in myself,
new mother,
this filling up of all my free moments
with tidying, scrubbing,
folding and refolding

as if untidiness
was the reason
he didn't want us

as if
I wasn't clean

Megan Buchannan

FOR PATRICK

O Scantron, swimming pool, poolhall genius!
All-American alcoholic,
heroic heartbreak, my brother.
How to fit
your surfer's shoulders,
your red '66 Bonneville, your relapses,
Jesuit diplomas and scholarships, trips to the pawnshop,
your sandy feet, your discreet knightly manner
and magnificent grin,
your seven-hundred-dollar hotel bar tab
in London last Christmas,
your off-the-ground and holy bearhugs
with tattooed forearms, all shamrocks, sparrows and saints,
and your secrets, submerged
beneath quicksilver tears
and all that cheap beer—-
how to fit you, little brother,
into this poem?

I'd love to write an ode as lyrical as you are,
moving through water with ball or board.
The formal, elevated style of an ode fits you perfectly
like a tuxedo or Speedo. You're dangerous
in either one; ask any one of my friends.
But let's get back to the poem
and its dignified theme
which, in this case, is death.
Tonight I'm awake late
afraid you might really die,
that the drink might pull you finally under
like the ocean does her lovers sometimes,
little brother, adrift.

You were born just before my first birthday.
I once could outrun you and later
outdrink you but not for long.
I really don't know you, the kid
across the teeter-totter
or the dinner table, napkins in our laps,
the kid behind me, holding tight to my T-shirt
astride the pony's back. I don't know
the serious man in the black motorcycle jacket
across the airplane aisle, reading a good magazine.
I don't know you,
I cannot put you back on the pony,
can't fit you into three stanzas,
can't save you

David Budbill

WHENEVER

Whenever I do the last things for the year,
like smoke the last bunch of sausages or
load the woodshed or the first things of the
year like defrost the freezer on a sub-zero
night in January, as we did last night—we
put all the freezer contents out on the porch
so they'll stay colder than if they'd been in
the freezer at ten below—I wonder if this
will be the last time.

David Budbill

Reply to My Peripatetic Friends

Why would I want to go anywhere? I'm already here.
—Lewis Hill, Horticulturist

I go to the waterfall
and listen to the water fall.

I sit on a rock
and stare at the sky.

I watch my self disappear
into the world around me.

Julie Cadwallader Staub

MILK

This goat kicked me only once,
as if to say she knows
I'm an amateur

but leaning my head
against her rounding flank,
I love the way her need for release

matches my need for her milk,
and I remember the ferocious little mouths
that latched on to me
relieving that overwhelming, dripping pressure of too much

and it was all too much then—
the endless stream of groceries meals
bills illnesses laundry jobs no sleep—
so to sit in the rocking chair was sweet respite,
to do just one thing:
watch the baby
drain the profusion of milk out of me
watch the baby
become so contented that nursing faded into sleep.

Now, this ordinary chore of milking generates
a similar contentment in me
the way her steady animal warmth warms me
the way my hands learn the ancient rhythm
the way the pail rings every time her milk hits it.

And a twinge of astonishment
quickens in me as well—
after you and I labored long and hard,
after we created so much together that is still so good—

how can it be that you didn't live long enough
to come round to this side
where simple contentment gives birth to joy.

Julie Cadwallader Staub

MEASUREMENT

I slept from 10 P.M. last night until 8:27 this morning.
Ten hours and twenty-seven minutes.
Yesterday I drove 328 miles to visit my sister in Princeton, N.J.
the home of Albert Einstein
who captured energy, mass and the speed of light
in an elegant equation that every student learns.

Look at us:
we quantify everything we can
in this complex and astonishing world,
from nanoseconds to eons
from millimeters to miles
from basis points to billions.

But no one can measure the velocity of hope,
        the way hope hatches
        fully fledged—in fact, already flying—
        between one word and the next
        between one breath and the next.

Neither can we calculate the stain of fear,
        the way it infects a childhood
        and spreads to a lifetime.

And we can only try to imagine the circumference of compassion
        the way it shows us the shape of love
        embracing, expanding,
        factoring in forgiveness
        it invents its own quantum leap,
        its own speed of light.

Hayden Carruth (Honorary Poet Laureate of Vermont, 2000)

EMERGENCY HAYING

Coming home with the last load I ride standing
on the wagon tongue, behind the tractor
in hot exhaust, lank with sweat,

my arms strung
awkwardly along the hayrack, cruciform.
Almost 500 bales we've put up

this afternoon, Marshall and I.
And of course I think of another who hung
like this on another cross. My hands are torn

by baling twine, not nails, and my side is pierced
by my ulcer, not a lance. The acid in my throat
is only hayseed. Yet exhaustion and the way

my body hangs from twisted shoulders, suspended
on two points of pain in the rising
monoxide, recall that greater suffering.

Well, I change grip and the image
fades. It's been an unlucky summer. Heavy rains
brought on the grass tremendously, a monster crop,

but wet, always wet. Haying was long delayed.
Now is our last chance to bring in
the winter's feed, and Marshall needs help.

We mow, rake, bale, and draw the bales
to the barn, these late, half-green,
improperly cured bales; some weigh 150 pounds

or more, yet must be lugged by the twine
across the field, tossed on the load, and then
at the barn unloaded on the conveyor

and distributed in the loft. I help—
I, the desk-servant, word-worker—
and hold up my end pretty well too; but God,

the close of day, how I fall down then. My hands
are sore, they flinch when I light my pipe.
I think of those who have done slave labor,

less able and less well prepared than I.
Rose Marie in the rye fields of Saxony,
her father in the camps of Moldavia

and the Crimea, all clerks and housekeepers
herded to the gaunt fields of torture. Hands
too bloodied cannot bear

even the touch of air, even
the touch of love. I have a friend
whose grandmother cut cane with a machete

and cut and cut, until one day
she snicked her hand off and took it
and threw it grandly at the sky. Now

in September our New England mountains
under a clear sky for which we're thankful at last
begin to glow, maples, beeches, birches

in their first color. I look
beyond our famous hayfields to our famous hills,
to the notch where the sunset is beginning,

then in the other direction, eastward,
where a full new-risen moon like a pale
medallion hangs in a lavender cloud

beyond the barn. My eyes
sting with sweat and loveliness. And who
is the Christ now, who

if not I? It must be so. My strength
is legion. And I stand up high
on the wagon tongue in my whole bones to say

woe to you, watch out
you sons of bitches who would drive men and women
to the fields where they can only die.

Hayden Carruth

Cows at Night

The moon was like a full cup tonight,
too heavy, and sank in the mist
soon after dark, leaving for light

faint stars and the silver leaves
of milkweed beside the road,
gleaming before my car.

Yet I like driving at night
in summer and in Vermont:
the brown road through the mist

of mountain-dark, among farms
so quiet, and the roadside willows
opening out where I saw

the cows. Always a shock
to remember them there, those
great breathings close in the dark.

I stopped, and took my flashlight
to the pasture fence. They turned
to me where they lay, sad

and beautiful faces in the dark,
and I counted them—forty
near and far in the pasture,

turning to me, sad and beautiful
like girls very long ago
who were innocent, and sad

because they were innocent,
and beautiful because they were
sad. I switched off my light.

But I did not want to go,
not yet, nor knew what to do
if I should stay, for how

in that great darkness could I explain
anything, anything at all.
I stood by the fence. And then

very gently it began to rain.

Hayden Carruth

LITTLE CITIZEN, LITTLE SURVIVOR

A brown rat has taken up residence with me.
A little brown rat with pinkish ears and lovely
almond-shaped eyes. He and his wife live
in the woodpile by my back door, and they are
so equal I cannot tell which is which when they
poke their noses out of the crevices among
the sticks of firewood and then venture farther
in search of sunflower seeds spilled from the feeder.
I can't tell you, my friend, how glad I am to see them.
I haven't seen a fox for years, or a mink, or
a fisher cat, or an eagle, or a porcupine, I haven't
seen any of my old company of the woods
and the fields, we who used to live in such
close affection and admiration. Well, I remember
when the coons would tap on my window, when
the ravens would speak to me from the edge of their
little precipice. Where are they now? Everyone knows.
Gone. Scattered in this terrible dispersal. But at least
the brown rat that most people so revile and fear
and castigate has brought his wife to live with me
again. Welcome, little citizen, little survivor.
Lend me your presence, and I will lend you mine.

David Cavanagh

The Ice Man

In 1991 he was found inside a glacier of the alps. Seems he had been out walking. An x-ray found an arrowhead in his back. He was 5,300 years old.

If he had known his stroll by an alpine lake
would be his last, how the arrow
from behind would thud into his daydream,
how the lake would claim him, harden,

how anthropologists would pore over
his Neolithic self the way his own kin
hovered with stone knives over a kill,
ready to skin, dismember, eat…

If he were fast-tracked five millennia,
would he say, what are you looking at,
what do you want to know, where fire
comes from? Or, hey, where can I

get some of those sneakers? Or, I am
no source, I am an omen. The way one
of us, blindsided, mangled by a muscle car
running the light, might face the Maker

calmly, nothing more to prove, might say,
I don't want in, just want you to know what
I've been through in case you want to learn
something. You gods, such know-it-alls.

Most of all, would he have wanted
a word with his mate left that morning
by a hearth? What tenderness, what worry
might have furrowed that big brow?

David Cavanagh

NEIL ARMSTRONG SHOOTS THE MOON

Neil Armstrong on his back deck
gazes up at the blatant moon
the way you might peer at a vacation photo
of Seattle propped on a cluttered
bookcase. Says, "I've been there." Or

Neil Armstrong shakes his bristled head,
"I've been THERE?" Same
as you, tossed in time, squint at all those
glossed Seattles floating
deep in inner space, far from your daily orbit.

Or even, like Neil, bathed in moondust,
feel the prick of small
skulking knowledge you've been there
but don't know the place
at all beyond a booted step on a crusty shell.

Or Neil says, "You know, I was only first
because I was sitting near
the door," and you recall a burbling phone
one tea-cozy morn,
all lunatic thereafter, a kettle whistling mad.

Or, if with a little launch of ego Neil says,
"I'VE been there," you wonder
what kind of "I" it was saw Seattle, and if
you still know that person
you know you badly need to know.

Or, less likely but to be hoped, Neil swivels
a craggy pate
up to the orange-yellow Buddha, feels
implausible rain or tears,
no telling which, kiss his runneled cheek.

Just as you, one ragged half-corked evening,
home in on the moonface
backlit in the bathroom mirror—so like
your father's, so much
stranger—gravely seeming to say,

"I've been watching
you for years. Time you noticed. Who
are you, really, what
is your intention, where have you been
to give off such a light?"

Dan Chiasson

Box and One

Here is our box-and-one:
the crucifix

an ice-pick in the back
of the wily point guard trooper's son.

Our press owes everything to Christ,
Our swish is the blood of sacrifice.

Last week we fucking killed St. Paul!

We're on defense inside my head.
The little synaptic me, No. 5
Guards a little synaptic forward

Inside the exact simulacrum
Of the Old Gym, eons later,
Now gooey with my brain matter—

And now the forward posts
And plants his feet—
Eureka! I had this thought:

To get a girl to flash her breasts
From her back patio,
First hold her cat hostage—

Then threaten the cat with fireworks
Aimed straight at its head . . .
So that was puberty: caught cat.

A pivot, another pivot, a pick—
He plays me tight
But I have my elation as my guide;

I have won not just any game;
A Cieplicki congratulates me.
I'll be in the Hall of Immortals.

I'll be immortal in the memory of men;
For writing poetry, I'll be
The poet equivalent of a Cieplicki.

&

(All rabbits in my poems are based
On an actual rabbit I caught,
cognoscente of Centennial Field

And thick ravine, never
the transparent eyeball,
ever the perv of Colchester Ave.)

&

What Thigpen wrought
Thigpen got

Linebacker
Southerner

Surrounded by rhymes
Inside this poem

Now he hides
Inside the void

Who lassoed me
Dim, kind, and drunk

Now I'm out of bounds.
Ten souls, numbered
And not one of them is me—

I try to inhere inside
A kayak bound
For Juniper Island

But find, instead, my psyche
In a mini-bonzai
In a wrecked terrarium—

(The cat was a Japanese maple;
The girl was my right fist;
The firecrackers were Seth's, anyway—

Nothing I say is true
Nor is it wrong to say
It's wrong to say—)

My grandfather had a depth finder,
He could find any walleye
In the breakwater of the lake,

It worked by radar no sonar
No Kevlar no Mylar
No anger no prayer

One day a walleye appeared
Upon the deck of his boat—
A sign from God, and edible—

That weekend's game I had
The calm of the elect,
As I smashed Christ the King

With my inimitable foulshot
And later feasted On the oracle, Ore-Ida.

･ᐧ

A sign from God who said:
Daniel, go inside
In the back of your blacklit closet

And commune with a magazine
And, lo, some later you
Years after, in the middle of his life's journey

Will peer over your shoulder
And wonder what it's like
Inside the inside of the covergirl.

･ᐧ

Ten souls, numbered.
Instinctively they play
The roles my memory assigns.

The wily one is always Hanzas.
It's always Aguiar's temper,
The jump-shot effloresces

Every time inside Lorenz's palm—
Ten souls and there I am—
No there, the shivering one,

St. Johnsbury: I'm sidelined;
I ventriloquize whatever man I become;
I emote like a hawk.
My vantage point is tree tops, prey.

Whatever I see, you see—

I have my famous throb already on!

Chin Woon Ping

Lola at Chow Time

—*for Joan Hutton Landis, Mistress of Rhyme*

slouched over bowl,
snouting like a bestial
feral, simple cur,
companion once to Hannibal
turned German normal,
clear as a deer's those eyes`
reflect trust phenomenal.
She stretches, crosses
front paws poised
as a Sphinx, she's Garbo,
Garland in disguise, almost
a lynx, a suit of red
and black fur hides
her keen tenderness.
Would I like Tathagata
of the Jataka leap
into the fire to feed
her fundamental need
for meat? She's Chong
to my Cheech,
bows and scrapes
for trifling treats
yet outstrips me
in sincerity.
What quiddity does she
define if not that
anonymous quip,
to err is human
to forgive, canine?

Chin Woon Ping

THE BEST PART OF THE LOBSTER IS

the head, of course
that samurai warrior helmet
of vivid vermillion
with its intricate secrets

that sturdy carapace
edged with tiny rows of tufted hairs
like mini-lashes or a bristly moustache

inside, a quivering film
of soft white custard more delicate
than the finest Ipoh tofu

Do they feel pain?
I ask the man hesitantly
Nah, they're nasty creatures

You eyed me back with black
beady eyes, Save me!
like you did the frogs
you bought in Singapore
at a busy restaurant

placed all seven in your backpack
as they thwacked insistently inside
drove them all the way to the mangrove
at Jurong Park, walked to the end

of the boardwalk, unzipped the pack
so they hopped out one by one:

Still afternoon
Frogs jump
Into the swamp

Michael Collier

Bronze Foot in a Glass Case: Damascus National Museum, 2007

Basra is a long way off. I walked there once,
along the Euphrates. When I say "I"
I mean this foot without a leg to lift it.
Step by step I marched.

After Basra, I returned to Palmyra,
City of Palms, and stood
a century or two in the shadow
of a wall, a foot with hundreds of feet

waiting for men of flesh and blood
to flood the city with violence,
killing everything that walked,
everything with legs and arms and heads.

If you, who are bending close to me,
can look through the glare
of your own reflection, you'll see
the layer of dust at my heel

and the shadows my toes cast
on the baize. This is where
the waiting ends, this is where
the violence recommences—,

in the dust and light
that gathers around me—you
who could not see it
until I told you to look.

Michael Collier

MY LAST MORNING WITH STEVE ORLEN

"Last Night I wrote a Russian novel or maybe it was English.
Either way, it was long and boring. My wife's laughter
might tell you which it was, and when she stops,
when she's not laughing, let's talk about the plot,
and its many colors. The blue that hovered in the door
where the lovers held each other but didn't kiss.
The red that by mistake rose in the sky with the moon,
and the moon-colored sun that wouldn't leave the sky.
All night I kept writing it down, each word arranged
in my mouth, but now, as you can see, I'm flirting
with my wife. I'm making her laugh. She's twenty.
I'm twenty-five, just as we were when we met, just
as we have always been, except for last night's novel,
Russian or English, with its shimmering curtain of color,
an unfading show of Northern Lights, what you, you asshole,
might call *Aurora Borealis*.
So sit down on the bed with my wife and me.
Faithful amanuensis, you can write down my last words,
not that they're great but maybe they are.
You wouldn't know. You're an *Aurora Borealis*.
But my wife is laughing and you're laughing too.
Just as we were at the beginning, just as we are at the end."

Jean Connor

OF SOME RENOWN

For some time now, I have
lived anonymously. No one
appears to think it's odd.
They think the old are,
well, what they seem. Yet
see that great egret

at the marsh's edge, solitary,
still? Mere pretense
that stillness. His silence is
a lie. In his own pond he is
of some renown, a stalker,
a catcher of fish. Watch him.

Jean Connor

One Morning

You could have said the clouds
were lifting or you could have said
the clouds were settling in over the long
low line of mountains, the day rich

with uncertainty. The world was silent
that morning, until the goats began
to bleat their complaints. A passerby,
who cared, strolled over to their pen,

calling out with cheerfulness, "Good morning,
goats! Good morning!" Then, she bowed
to them. And the young nun,
who knew the goats, laughed, and

went on with her sweeping, while humming
a song about being strong. After that,
I can't remember whether it rained
Or not, but everyone knew who he was.

The marigolds were marigolds
and the goats were goats, and we,
we felt no need to urge the zinnias
to be roses or anything else.

Wyn Cooper

On Eight Mile

She appears as if at the edge
of a screen, her brown hair black
in this light, her legs moving the way

she wants you to want them to move.
It's hard to see the woman you loved
dance naked in a room full of men

and come up to your table after
and ask for a light, and the light
in her eyes is still the same,

only her job has changed. So she changes
into clothes and we cross the street
to a quiet place where we can talk,

and the talk turns to me, to what
I do that makes me think I'm better
than her. I'm not and I know it,

but she won't be convinced. Nothing
I can say will sway her the way
she sways on stage. And nothing

can make me look away.

Wyn Cooper

Mars Poetica

Imagine you're on Mars, looking at earth,
a swirl of colors in the distance.
Tell us what you miss most, or least.

Let your feelings rise to the surface.
Skim that surface with a tiny net.
Now you're getting the hang of it.

Tell your story slantwise,
streetwise, in the disguise
of an astronaut in his suit.

Tell us something we didn't know
before: how words mean things
we didn't know we knew.

Stephen Cramer

COLD WAS THE GROUND

A moan dragged across
      gravel, a guitar's metallic
complaint & shimmy—

these sounds rattle the zodiac,
      wail to the mute eruption

& flare of a collapsing star. *Dark*
      was the Night, Cold
was the Ground

by Blind Willie Johnson—
      3 minutes & 15 seconds

of bruised spiritual—
      is touring the cosmos
alongside *The Brandenburg*

Concerto & *Johnny*
      B. Goode on the spacecraft

Voyager, the music flanked
      by a slew of natural sounds:
surf & thunder, crickets,

a kiss, a heartbeat—
      an aural primer

to planet Earth. The world
      is phonic. What's matter—
blueberry, backhoe, the back

of your hand—but the shards
      of that primeval sound

when the universe
　　　　detonated from the ghost
of a pebble?

On this journey,
　　　　any *one* man's history

is dwarfed
　　　　by boundless gulf
& pulsar—Voyager,

long past Pluto,
　　　　is 100,000 years

from the next system—
　　　　but here you are
on Earth & so it matters

that when Johnson was 7,
　　　　his stepmother, aiming

for his father, cast lye
　　　　into his face, the price
for his father's infidelity.

Blinded, he was resigned
　　　　to a street corner: the dull

rattle of tips pooling
　　　　in a cup, a woman passing
to another running catalogue

of bouquets—husk of sweat, at first,
　　　　then salt, then almonds—

her body's continuous assertions
　　　　grown hyperbolic. He could
smell moods—their delicate

swerves evident as each
        nuance of skin's pit & swell—

smell the fur
        before it brushed his arm,
before the woman backed away

in a clatter of heels.
                Years later, he could smell

the stench of soaked char
        in the ruined pit
of his house. Turned away

from the hospital after the fire
        that gutted his roof,

he returned to a rain-soaked
        bed of newspaper & soot,
& pneumonia killed him

in the ashes,
        beneath a ceiling

not of wood or plaster
        but of stars.
What are blues

with no human to hear?
        What's a kiss

or a heartbeat
        to that grand sweep

of interplanetary ash
        but molecules bumping
molecules? Stranger, unimaginable

intergalactic pilgrim
        who's never even heard
of a tongue,

if you've found this note
        curled in our million dollar can,

hear the absurdity of our glory
        & our pain. Transmute it
into we know not what:

space dust, star kindling.
        Restore us back to sound.

Stephen Cramer

WHAT WE DO

A metallic detonation arcs
      over Broadway's gulf, & the aluminum
            contorts to contain the continuous
syncopation wrecked into its side—

with two feet of pipe
      a man's beating a keg till it turns useless
            for anything else but to carry
his liquid rhythms. He's drumming

a rim full of dents, angled
      facets that pull to themselves
            all the sun they can bear before tossing
a tremolo of light off the bricks behind.

Look around: whatever this sound is
      that ricochets the streets is contagious—
            less drums than a seasonal quickening
that everything's so busy keeping up with,

new desire mixing up the thick torpor
      of the past months. At my feet,
            two pigeons struggle over any spare
piece of garbage to entice a female.

They fumble in this patch of spilled popcorn,
      gurgling and churring in figure-eights,
            inflating the sheen of their necks
over their turf. Even when she dodges

away, they just keep flashing iridescence
      for no one. Noontime, the drummer's checking
            the metal where he's reflected
in more than one place, tucking a stray

curl behind his ear. But just so you don't
        forget whose block this is,
                when a woman goes by
he's sent demonic, like he knows

this commotion's for keeps,
        and he's thrown into a shimmy
                of the hips which he rises out of
just in time to fit the mechanical stumble

of a far off jackhammer into his running
        cadence. These sounds the music *wants*
                to encompass, make its own,
so in the end, you can't tell if he's playing

the drums or if they're playing him.
        Because when you're itching
                to finish with your wrists
the rumble that begins in your gut,

this is what you do—you're ready
        to bang on *anything* for love.
                You'll break your hands
to get that rhythm out.

Dede Cummings

LAMENT OF THE GLACIERS

> *. . . for not even the flutter of a fly's wing*
> *is as fast as change.*
> —SIMONIDES OF CEOS

I pray to the final human being
on earth,
the last one standing,
on the edge of what once was
thick blue gray ice the size
of Manhattan. She is not
wrapped in fur, but laced
with claw marks from ivory talons;
she squints through cataracts,
tormented by what remains
of what was once a frozen sea,
to find a precipice; she
drops to all fours,
looks around, and panting
from the effort,
throws a stone
in the direction
of the wind.

Dede Cummings

FALLING GROUNDS

The ride down Bonnyvale is always swift, the barn and horses
at Meg's farm
stare at the bike blur of me, cows down by Dutton's snort
as they lie down.
The bike whizzes by, and I am not really the rider at this early hour.

By Irene's house, I see she has her laundry out.
The two reddish squares,
quilts hanging, are the equivalent of Tibetan prayer flags for me,
as I note the date
that my father would have turned eighty-three. A cool snap
is in the air.
Put the bike down, fossil from another era, fuel
from a zero-emission vehicle.

"Write what you know," Mr. Carruth's pipe hangs on his lower lip.
"Why don't you write me a poem that will prepare me
for your death?"

So this is what I was thinking when I climbed the ladder
to the topmost branches of our apple tree. The red bruises
stare out at me.
The tartness of the ripened fruit dries my mouth immediately,
the picking is what is worth doing, the straw basket by my side
is weighted down,
the ache in my shoulder is a cause for celebration.

Gregory Djanikian

BANALITY

There's something to be said for banality,
the way it keeps everything on a level plane,
one cliché blithely following another
like cows heading toward the pasture.

How lovely sometimes not to think
about Russian Futurism, or the second law
of thermodynamics, or how thinking itself
requires some thoughtfulness.

I'd like to ask if Machiavelli
ever owned a dog named "Prince."
I'd like to imagine Rosalind Franklin
lounging pleasantly by a wood stove.

Let the mind take a holiday,
the body put its slippers on.
It's a beautiful day, says the banal,
and today, I'm happy to agree
with its genial locutions.

Woof, woof, goes the neighbor's dog.
The sun is pouring in through the window,
heating up the parlor, the blue sky is so blue,
and the cumulous clouds are looking very cumulous.

I'm all for reading a murder mystery,
something with flair but forgettable.
Or some novelette whose hero's name
is Hawk or Kestrel, a raptor bird
soaring above his ravished love.

I'm lying on the couch with easy puzzles.
I'm playing a song that has no accidentals.
Life's but a dream, comme ci, comme ça.

No doubt, tomorrow I'll be famished
for what's occult and perilous,
all those knots in the brain,
all the words that are hard to crack.

Today, I'm floating like a feather,
call me Falcon, look me up
in the field guide under Blissful,
Empty-headed, under everything
that loves what it does today,
and requires no explanation.

Gregory Djanikian

Mystery Farm Road

You don't know how you've gotten here
what accidental turn on the road you took
while thinking hardly of anything

but here you are suddenly at a river
shaded by black willows on either bank,
the water dark and indecipherable,

and it is this river, you are sure,
that ran through the book you read one summer
as a boy in Alexandria

when the plains of Kansas were as far away
as you are now from your childhood.
And you feel a certain dizziness

as you see the railroad tracks running
along the river, and the small bridge
you've kept inside you all these years,

and the red barn on the other side
with its silver roof shining
like a vision of America.

How sure you are that the freight train
on its way west will soon pass through here
sounding its long plaintive whistle

or that the school bus you've always
wanted to ride through the waves of grain
will appear over the crest.

The book in your memory is riffling
its pages, whispering to you
though you can't remember the beginning or end,

only the farm, which is before you,
and a dog howling at the passing trains,
and a boy standing by a river,

and now another boy in Alexandria
on Rue Ahmed Shawky, reading a book
and mouthing the words *huckleberry* and *harvest*

that will cast a spell on him
for years, and that boy is you,
and the boy by the river

baring his calves under the black willows
is also you, look at him wading in, throwing
handfuls of water to the sky.

Greg Delanty

LOOSESTRIFE

You have become your name, loosestrife,
        carried on sheep, spurting up out of ballast,
a cure brought across the deep
        to treat wounds, soothe trouble.
There have been others like you, the rhododendron,
        the cattails that you in your turn overrun.
Voices praise your magenta spread, your ability
        to propagate by seed, by stem, by root
and how you adjust to light, to soil, spreading
        your glory across the earth even as you kill
by boat, by air, by land all before you: the hardy iris,
        the rare orchids, the spawning ground of fish.
You'll overtake the earth and destroy even yourself.
        Ah, our loosestrife, purple plague, beautiful us.

Greg Delanty

The Alien

I'm back again scrutinizing the Milky Way
    of your ultrasound, scanning the dark
        matter, the nothingness, that now the heads say
    is chockablock with quarks & squarks,
gravitons and gravitini, photons & photinos. Our sprout,

who art there inside the spacecraft
    of your Ma, the time capsule of this printout,
        hurling and whirling towards us, it's all daft
    on this earth. Our alien who art in the heavens,
our Martian, our little green man, we're anxious

to make contact, to ask divers questions
    about the heavendom you hail from, to discuss
        the whole shebang of the beginning & end,
    the pre-big bang untime before you forget the why
& lie of thy first place. And, our friend,

to say Welcome, that we mean no harm, we'd die
    for you even, that we pray you're not here
        to subdue us, that we'd put away
    our ray guns, missiles, attitude and share
our world with you, little big head, if only you stay.

Chard deNiord (Vermont Poet Laureate, 2015-2019)

By The Sweat Of My Face

For Maxine Kumin

Part may be more than whole, least may be best.
——Robert Francis
Earth, is it not just this that you want: to arise invisibly in us?
Is not your dream to be one day invisible? Earth! invisible!
——Rainer Maria Rilke

I made a list for each day,
which was enough, since I was inclined
to do too much in a single day—
more than a dozen men sometimes
in a couple of days, so drawn to work
and blessed with strength I couldn't imagine
paradise without it, much less remember
the bliss that idlers canonized
as myth more real than the history of days.
"Fix the bridge, weed the beans,
till the corn, plant some chard,"
I wrote in the box of my birthday,
which in the rule of night became
an order for that day, like all
the other days that authorized
my sleep to grant me another
day as long as I saw the ruse
of difference between each thing,
then woke with the charge of putting my mind
to the dream, which was my work
in the garden, the plot that needed me
and not the other in rows of text
that merely bloomed. To be the genius
of my own patch with only so
many days to plant, grow,

and reap. So, I gathered my tools at dawn
and headed down to the field and jacked
the bridge that had fallen in the rains.
Placed a stone the ground had made
a million years ago for this
repair beneath the beam that had lost
its hold on the opposite bank. Weeded
the beans until it was time to rest,
then sat for a while in the shade of a willow
beside the stream. Thought about nothing
until it was something as part of the whole
that was also whole for being connected
to the most unlikely things: ant,
pokeweed, mullein, worm…Stuck
my head in the stream like a lure for the big one
that always gets away. Walked
back to the garden to till the corn
only to find the corpse of a mouse
inside the case that houses the machine.
Back up then to fetch the ratchet
and a little shroud to bury her in—
slower this time than before
and grievous now—one dead at least
and maybe more from catching against
the screen when I pulled the cord and it
pulled back. "Poor mousie," I cried
like Burns. I should have guessed some creature
was there after finding a snake last year
wound round and round the sprocket
like another cord. So many dead
inside the tiller. So much work
recovering the bodies. *House, housing,*
mouse, bridge, fountain, snake,
I thought like the sky whose clouds
erase its blues so perfectly.
Like the dirt that smells of the hole
and everything in it. Words were all;

they came to me like birds to a tree
and I wrote them down for nothing
with a trowel for the stars to scan as nothing
also—so much nothing at the end
of the day I called it darling, darling.

Chard deNiord

To Hear And Hear

The hermit thrush is set for six
to sing her song, as if it were
the end of the world and she was stirred
by dusk to sing the same sweet song
again and again in the understory,
as if to say, it's neither words
nor meaning that matter in the end
but the quality of sound, as if we
were deafened by the sun and needed
her song as a key to unlock our ears,
to hear and hear and understand,
to see and see, knowing that this
one day is the end for now,
which it is, *it is,* she claims, with a song
just loud enough to pierce the woods
until the night descends like a thousand
veils, and then just one.

Chard deNiord

THE STAR OF "INTERSTATE"

The clouds were curtains that parted onto the show
of sky above the scar of 89.
Oh, the big blue screen of autumn days
and score that featured mainly strings.
                              Oh,
the epic *Something, Then Nothing* that opened as
a matinee but played into the night
on a single reel inside the room that housed
the machine.
              I drove with one eye open and the other
closed.
          I couldn't tell if the things I was seeing—
broken line, blinking light, leaping
deer—were live or frozen frames.
                              Were on
the road or in my mind, into which
I'd also driven at a dangerous speed.
I was bearing down in the passing lane inside
the theater of my Chevrolet.
                          I was seeing
myself through the lens of a windshield in the opposite
lane.
        I could smell the sky with the windows closed.
I could hear her voice from every cloud, "Come home,
my love. Come home."
                      I believed there was still a way,
despite my fame as *the man who flies,* to return
as myself some day and give her the keys.

Chard deNiord

CHAINS

I took the chains down to the hardware store
to have them sharpened on the grinding wheel.
It was the day before the day of rest, so I worked
some more when I returned, gathering branches
into a pile, starting a fire, tending the flames
until they disappeared at dawn and I went inside
to lie with her, the Queen of Trees, who had waited
for me throughout the night, breathing her lullaby
now beneath the quilt, emitting the sweet
eternal scent of the future against my stench,
leading me with her beauty alone into the dark
where I dreamed of the trees I felled still falling
in that slow intractable way they fall at first,
then faster in their swift descent that takes forever
it seems despite their speed since in the time
between the second the tree begins to fall
and the moment it hits the ground, a man has time
to write his epitaph on the stone inside his head
and lay some flowers as well on the mound that rises
up before him like a wave wherever he stands.

Mary Jane Dickerson

Mother's Body

at ninety-five still moves
with a stateliness
as she steps into her bath
while I, her handmaiden now,
encircle her waist with my arms
to steady her as she eases herself
into the waiting warmth of water.

Shoulders always erect, breasts
sloping toward a waist that's
never lost its inward curve, flesh
like white satin and cool to the touch,
she still moves with the grace
of Bathsheba as she once stood poised
before lowering herself into the bath,
or Susanna disrobed by her maidens at pool's edge
before entering the soothing waters—figures of females
always vulnerable in that intimate moment
of immersing themselves into
the transparency of water.

Mary Jane Dickerson

Before the Interstate

Before the interstate, the drive
from Jericho to Norwich was a trip
on roads now called "back roads":
Routes 100, 2, 114 and 5 that wound
around and through towns and villages
with names like Waterbury, Randolph,
Sharon, and Northfield, with signs pointing
toward Jerusalem and Dowdey Corner,
roads and byways that did not bore
through the Green Mountain range
but made their way up and down and then around
in a leisurely design that made getting there
the work of much of a day with, in favorable
weather, the occasional picnic spread
in an empty pasture to break up the journey.
Before the interstate, cows ambling along,
crossing the road from pasture to pasture
or from pasture to barn for milking, meant
long minutes to count the members of the herd,
whether in those days Guernsey or Jersey,
time aplenty to study the dairy farms—some with pastures
rambling up a rocky hillside, others with meadows
and low-lying fields along the Winooski's banks—
barns with milking parlors and silage mounded against silos,
machinery hulking about the barnyard, the white clapboard
or red brick farmhouse a measured distance from the barn,
its smoke in winter rising straight from the chimney
through wisps of clouds into the blueness beyond.
Before the interstate, no matter the season,
traveling often meant more than distances covered,
taking us through more than the late spring day
that began in sunshine, moved through thickening clouds
with bursts of rain or even sleet

falling in a noisy curtain over the car,
before ending with large wet snowflakes dissolving
into the air as they slowly drifted onto pavement
stretching far into what lay ahead.

    Yet, what we may miss most from before
the interstate—more even than the villages along the way
with people moving about in the day-to-day of their lives,
more than the weather always reminding us
we were still in Vermont—was what drifted
in from the car's open windows:
the spring-time skunk caught crossing the road,
the life-giving air infusing smells given off
by the land itself when families turned out to mow,
then bale and bring in the hay to sweeten the barn
and by the animals grazing on the hillsides,
especially the richly pungent odor of manure
being spread in fields or wafting from cows
on their methodical and measured steps
crossing the road, impervious to our gaze.

Norman Dubie

ORATION: HALF-MOON IN VERMONT

A horse is shivering flies off its ribs, grazing
Through the stench of a sodden leachfield.

On the broken stairs of a trailer
A laughing fat girl in a T-shirt is pumping
Milk from her swollen breasts, cats
Lapping at the trails. There's a sheen of rhubarb
On her dead fingernail. It's a humid morning.

Tonight, with the moon washing some stars away,
She'll go searching for an old bicycle in the shed;
She'll find his father's treasures:
Jars full of bent nails, a lacquered bass,
And the scythe with spiders
Nesting in the emptiness of the blade
And in the bow of its pine shaft.
Milling junk in the dark,

She'll forget the bicycle, her getaway,
And rescue
A color photograph of an old matinee idol.
Leaving the shed, she'll startle

An owl out on the marsh. By November
It will be nailed through the breast to the barn.

In a year the owl will go on a shelf in the shed
Where in thirty years there will be a music box
Containing a lock of hair, her rosaries,
Her birth certificate,

And an impossibly sheer, salmon-pink scarf. What
I want to know of my government is

Doesn't poverty just fucking break your heart?

Norman Dubie

A FIFTEENTH-CENTURY ZEN MASTER

for Stephen

A blind girl steps over the red staves
Of a tub. Steam rising from her shoulders and hair,
She walks across a dirt floor to you.
I think you are not her grandfather.
You watch with her a pink man
Who has avoided taxes for two winters—
He is being judged by roosters
And has been chased this far into the countryside. Above him

Burning sacks of bat dung are arranged
In the purple branches of the thistle trees.
The river is indifferent to him.
And so are we.
You tell your mistress the burning bags of shit
Are like inert buddhas
Dissolving in a field of merit.

She giggles. A front tooth is loose.
With the river bottom clear as the night air,
The bargeman sings through the hungry vapors
Rising now like white snakes behind him.
You told his wife that Lord Buddha made wasps
From yellow stalks of tobacco with a dark spit.

Down in the cold bamboo a starving woman
Has opened a small pig—
The old moons climb from its blue glistening stomach,
Or is it light
From the infinitely receding sacks of shit?

Master, where is the difference?

Ellen Dudley

On The Mill Race

A pair of great blue herons in the dead cherry last night
and as dusk came on in rain and sleet,
the wail of a loon sailed across the pond
out from among the canadas, mergansers and a grebe or two.
Here in the lilacs, not three feet from my window,
a ruby-crowned kinglet, then another
and a yellow shafted flicker on our lawn—
the lawn that once belonged to MacNighter
and before that Fletcher—and our old cats
buried out there beneath this spring's mud.

Where the old barn stood, where the soil is good from
years of pigs and cattle, where the brown mutt followed
MacNighter to the barn in a spring blizzard
to watch over the early calf in the stall, warm and steamy
of a March night. And on the overturned bucket
by the door, the old man stroked the yellow tiger,
as on the back porch we built years later, I stroked
the black-and-white who would go missing
that next winter, but this night purred
as the August Perseids fell down
and tanks filled the streets of Moscow.

And MacNighter and Fletcher and those before—
the orange cat, the boy lost in Belgium and another
in the next war. The spring hopeful with calves,
the milk hitting the bucket with a ping
and in the milk can's top, warm liquid for the cat
and the purr filling the barn.

Or August, here, years later with the cat
and the peepers and the bullfrogs and the voice
calling from the lighted house: "Where are you?"
And "Come in."

Ellen Dudley

THE CENTURY PLANT

Agave. Gray-green plant whose leaves
if they can be called that, not swords or bayonets,
fling themselves up and out. Plant them
beneath your window to keep the burglars away:
a roofer, falling in a copse, grove, bunch
of them, spent three months in critical
care—the things passed right through him.
Oh but we love them, love a plant because it grows
huge and strong, because it shoots up blossoms
phallic and thick as tree trunks, but most
because its life span, we like to think,
mimics ours.
                            It blooms. It dies.
Then we have the backhoe come and dig
the damned thing up. An American plant, spending
itself in the theatrical gesture of bloom. Look,
we say, a baby. A small agave has sprouted from
the seed of the dead. It's as big as a dinner plate.
It will outlive us.

John Engels

BARKING DOG

From down the road and near the landlord's house
his terrible dog, whose fierce and guardian voice
kept us all close upon our boundaries,
warmed up with a few preliminary snarls,
then barked, savage, incurious, and untiring
the whole night: two sharp yelps, a pause,
and then unvarying two more—nor could I sleep.
Therefore, though I disliked at night
to walk through my over-dark and speechless house
where I must pass a room in which lurked
some uncommon terror that once
had come to someone who lived in my house
there in that room, and died; and then to walk
along the cold, light-feeding road;
nevertheless I ventured out
into the dog-voiced night, angry to be afraid,
when just at the corner of our properties
the world fell silent, and a great black dog
charged across the yard. He was silent,
he seemed not tentative, he carried
his head low. Of all the dread forms,
most I dreaded that! Slowly I backed away
afraid to turn, our eyes on one another's, till
I thought I might be safe, and flung about and ran.
Thank God he did not follow, only
all night ranged the bench marks of our yards
and barked, and barked. This happened long ago
when I was wary of malice, large and small,
convinced, though nothing could I see, that I was seen,
and had not journeyed far in understanding
whichever way I turned was always something
at my back. How was it they who lived
along the landlord's road and in his house
had borne it that long while, that voice

which overwhelmed the world,
strict of measure and extensive of dominion,
and they lived nearer than ever I lived? Thus
in the large world peace has not yet visited!
For his voice which troubled me was strong and large,
and carried far, and nothing drowned it out;
for so was set his measure in my head.

John Engels

Green Bay Flies

Two deep rivers ran deep
through the heart of town to the Bay,
And in March I watched the ice break up
and the big floes go tumbling, splintering
the piers, debarking the oaks and pines
along the banks four feet up their trunks.
In April, the first thunder
in six months, proclaiming
spring, and in July
up from the Bay, from beyond
Peet's Slough and Long Tail Point
and the marsh meadows blue
with sweet flag the hatch came,
a fly or two fluttering
to the street lights, than a few more, then
before you knew it
the mayflies of Green Bay would be swarming up
the Fox in hugh rustling clouds half as wide
as the river, so many they darkened the arc lights
on the Blue Jays' field, covered
every window pane, clustered the screens, clogged
car radiators, covered your hat, your sleeves
sometimes even brought traffic
to a halt. You could feel their wings
brushing your face with littles breezes
that I swear were enough
to cool you down on a hot night, the air
adazzle with wings, and high
in the evening sky swallows
by the hundreds, cedar waxwings
darting out from the trees to meet a fly
just perfectly in mid flight, one second
this little fluttery dab of golden light,
then the flash and hover

of the bird, then
nothing,
like a flicked switch, the evening gone
minutely the darker for it.
If it had been raining
the streets and sidewalks in the morning
would be slippery with green slime
of eggs, the flies having mistaken
the wet concrete for a surface
of live water. But nothing
like it anymore, the hatch
is over, probably
forever, the Bay a soup
of silt and sewage and sulfides
from the mills, not even clean
enough to swim in anymore. But back then
those summer evenings—I can still
hear it, the sound
like a long train
way off in the distance,
a sort of humbling rumble
wrought up by those millions
billions, of delicate wings
that caught up every last scrap of light
left to the day in the last
half hour as night came down
and the street lamps
came on. I've never forgotten
how it was those years in July
the night stepping in, slow
and deliberate as a heron, the sky
softly darkening like it does
even now, evenings
in late summer, a smell
of lawns and dust and the steely
scent of the Bay drifting in, the air
still hot, but a growing softness
to everything—at such a time

you could surprise
yourself, catch sight of yourself
in a shop window, if the time
was right, and the mayflies
hadn't yet swarmed the glass, and depending
on how you wanted to look to yourself,
in such a light you'd look it.

Alvin Feinman

November Sunday Morning

And the light, a wakened heyday of air
Tuned low and clear and wide,
A radiance now that would emblaze
And veil the most golden horn
Or any entering of a sudden clearing
To a standing, astonished, revealed . . .

That the actual streets I loitered in
Lay lit like fields, or narrow channels
About to open to a burning river;
All brick and window vivid and calm
As though composed in a rigid water
No random traffic would dispel . . .

As now through the park, and across
The chill nailed colors of the roofs,
And on near trees stripped bare,
Corrected in the scant remaining leaf
To their severe essential elegance,
Light is the all-exacting good,

That dry, forever virile stream
That wipes each thing to what it is,
The whole, collage and stone, cleansed
To its proper pastoral . . .

I sit And smoke, and linger out desire
And know if I closed my eyes I'd hear
Again what held me awake all night
Beside her breathing: a rain falling
It seemed into a distant stillness,
On broad low leaves beside a pond
And drop upon drop into black waters.

Alvin Feinman

The Way to Remember Her

Take only this, the hand, the flower
In her hand, imagine, do not look,
Her eyes, her lips, call that delight—
      And burn the name of it.

Dispel the reasons from your lips
And what it comes to, lips, and eyes,
The held flower always in the end—
      And burn the name of it.

And tear from what your voice intends
The word it tells you or the thought
Reminds, beginning, end, again—
      And burn the name of it.

—Or burn that hand, the lips,
The eyes, the flower, all, all save
The knowledge, the desire that kills
And leaves the burning name of it.

Kate Fetherston

A Killing Frost

is forecast in the meadow where summer
opened full and fell, where my peonies drifted
hip deep, round as vowels. Now the garden's

stubble, and my mouth's a blood cloudbellied
bruise. I taste the unspent metal tang
of coming snow. How I long to lie

with you in May's neglected apple trees, their backs
long bent to old grandmothers that cradle
the naked flowers. Oh, for July rain to catch us weeding

unruly iris, August light to tuck us in, sloe-eyed
deer searching out sweet! Your quiet arms, the sleep-
heavy insects moaning their indecipherable

trance dance in blackberry bushes. What
indolence, what honey the green scented earth
of your tongue! But today you and I

wake slowly to a keening chaff-dulled blade;
we rise as November's scrap-heap clamors over
the window sill of the house of the hour

of the bed of our lives. And behind weary
eyelids, my familiar demon lays a frigid
finger on my heart and whispers, *Drink now*

winter's word-poor draught where you'll
fall empty and alone as snow. Memory belongs
to the living. You'll not outlive your life.

Kate Fetherston

Take Bitter For Sweet

Each poem a stranger shanghais us sleep
drunk into a rickshaw rattling through this small

town dawn—incongruous
and alone with only our strangeness

for company. Yes, and under a sea of stars we fall
backward into our lives, from water

into water. I, half-witted insomniac, outside
in my robe at first light, attempt any negligible

truth, but, as usual, I'm not
equal to the task. Bleary, I stumble

into the honeysuckle bush whose silver leaves
cup orange and crimson berries. I measure

the weight of fruit in my hands, each
destiny held by nothing. Call it gravity, chance,

or family dynamics by whose impeccable
vertigo we navigate constellations drawn

from a game of pick-up sticks. Still,
the dust of the world is everywhere, luminous

as this air I'm breathing, while, upstairs in our bed
you're softly snoring, your unhappiness

blossoms over our pillows, its runnels
whisper my helplessness. All I have

to offer is a handful of saffron, plus a few
liquid notes from the finches shacking up in our

neglected apple tree. I say neglected, but
what I mean is, left to wildness and the love

I will surely die of. If every poem's a stranger,
then this dark form leans

against ghost light while a rickety
travois clattering

down an unlit street spills the loose
beads of my need

for you. The paperboy tosses today's bad
news at the neighbor's porch, as I

mingle my breath with yours, same
world, same cast of fools and angels

taking bitter for sweet. Isaiah the prophet
preached, *Woe to those who mistake*

gall for honey, day
for night, but my tongue

fills with brine and rose, apple
and ash, when I say life's

hard enough—let us make of it
what we can. This exile

calling you home.

Florence Fogelin

Reading, Writing, and Orthophony

> *Orthophony; or The Cultivation of the Voice in Elocution*
> William Russell, 39th edition, 1871

> *To persons whose habits are*
> *studious and sedentary, and especially*
> *to females, the vigorous exercise of the*
> *organs of respiration and of voice, is,*
> *in every point of view, an invaluable*
> *discipline.*

That poetry should come to this!
Garrison Keillor's celebration, mid-July,
Shall I compare thee to a summer's day. . . .
a lugubrious monotone ending lines in downspeak:
alas, the current sad-sack *poet's voice.*

Proper elocution was schooled with sentence examples,
Chapter I. Respiration, or Exercises in Breathing,
utterances low to high . . . . pitch . . . . stress . . . . force . . . .
impassioned, whispering, half-whispering . . . .

> *till he finds himself able, from*
> *a single glance at the first line of a*
> *piece, to determine its gradation of*
> *feeling, and its true note in utterance.*

You see a page of poetry
but can you listen to it? Synch your lips with it?
Say it, said Robert Frost. Say the poem,
even if it's memorized. Especially if it's memorized.
The poem shapes your mouth. It tells you where to breathe.
Practice breathing.

Florence Fogelin

All Men Are Mortal

∴

the
sign of
therefore,
of the cold logic
of why and what we
remember, what brought
us here: another war memorial,
another slant on death, the dead piled
into another pyramid, their names pressed
with salted fingers into granite. They were men;
all men are mortal. Did you think they'd live forever?
Between the *why* and *therefore* falls the shadow.

South and north of here,
on Southern courthouse lawns and Yankee greens,
black cannonballs kiss as much as need demands,

one

on three

three on six

six on ten & so on

death on death, as deliberate as war's careful explanation:
Reasons. Premises. Conclusion.
Washington's smooth face expresses a way to remember,
a why to forget.

Laura Foley

THE ORCHARD ON ITS WAY

I wish it would slow,
not the train, but the ponies
shivering in a rain-soaked pasture,
a hundred geese fluttering
in a soggy field,
the eagles' wild mating dance
we saw this morning
from a Vermont station—
not the train, but the passing
into memory—I want it all
to last, the chimney falling
back to bricks,
the orchard on its way to bud,
the kiss you gave me
twenty miles back.

Laura Foley

IT IS TIME

It is time to gather sticks of wood
so we can cook the sap that we have drawn from the earth.
We will bore holes into the maple trees,
collect buckets, stir the froth as it boils.
Then we'll finish it on the stove in the barn.
We will do this together,
balancing the heavy iron vat,
pouring the hot syrup,
tasting the sweetness.
We did it through the pregnancies, the births.
Let's do it once again.
And then we will cultivate the honey bees
and tend to the alfalfa in the fields.
It will be the best of times once more,
fourteen loads of fresh hay,
and my hair will be long and we will collect raspberries
and make a pie.
The garden will yield a bumper crop of beets and basil
and we will split wood all fall
and stack it
and be ready for the winter,
when you will weave a blanket on your loom
with dog hair and horse hair and my hair
and some dyed wool too.
And I will nurse the babies by the fire
and neither of us will grow older
and we will never forget
and nothing will ever die.
We need to gather sticks now
and build a fire quickly
before the season passes on
before the field
where you are sleeping
blossoms.

Robert Frost (Vermont Poet Laureate, 1961-1963)

CLOSED FOR GOOD

Much as I own I owe
The passers of the past
Because their to and fro
Has cut this road to last,
I owe them more today
Because they've gone away

And not come back with steed
And chariot to chide
My slowness with their speed
And scare me to one side.
They have found other scenes
For haste and other means.

They leave the road to me
To walk in saying naught
Perhaps but to a tree
Inaudibly in thought,
"From you the road receives
A priming coat of leaves.

"And soon for lack of sun
The prospects are in white
It will be further done,
But with a coat so light
The shape of leaves will show
Beneath the brush of snow."

And so on into winter
Till even I have ceased
To come as a foot printer,
And only some slight beast
So mousy or so foxy
Shall print there as my proxy.

Robert Frost

IRIS BY NIGHT

One misty evening, one another's guide,
We two were groping down a Malvern side
The last wet fields and dripping hedges home.
There came a moment of confusing lights,
Such as according to belief in Rome
Were seen of old at Memphis on the heights
Before the fragments of a former sun
Could concentrate anew and rise as one.
Light was a paste of pigment in our eyes.
And then there was a moon and then a scene
So watery as to seem submarine;
In which we two stood saturated, drowned.
The clover-mingled rowan on the ground
Had taken all the water it could as dew,
And still the air was saturated too,
Its airy pressure turned to water weight.
Then a small rainbow like a trellis gate,
A very small moon-made prismatic bow,
Stood closely over us through which to go.
And then we were vouchsafed a miracle
That never yet to other two befell
And I alone of us have lived to tell.
A wonder! Bow and rainbow as it bent,
Instead of moving with us as we went
(To keep the pots of gold from being found),
It lifted from its dewy pediment
Its two mote-swimming many-colored ends
And gathered them together in a ring.
And we stood in it softly circled round
From all division time or foe can bring
In a relation of elected friends.

Robert Frost

THE DRAFT HORSE

With a lantern that wouldn't burn
In too frail a buggy we drove
Behind too heavy a horse
Through a pitch-dark limitless grove.

And a man came out of the trees
And took our horse by the head
And reaching back to his ribs
Deliberately stabbed him dead.

The ponderous beast went down
With a crack of a broken shaft.
And the night drew through the trees
In one long invidious draft.

The most unquestioning pair
That ever accepted fate
And the least disposed to ascribe
Any more than we had to to hate,

We assumed that the man himself
Or someone he had to obey
Wanted us to get down
And walk the rest of the way.

Robert Frost

Wild Grapes

What tree may not the fig be gathered from?
The grape may not be gathered from the birch?
It's all you know the grape, or know the birch.
As a girl gathered from the birch myself
Equally with my weight in grapes, one autumn,
I ought to know what tree the grape is fruit of.
I was born, I suppose, like anyone,
And grew to be a little boyish girl
My brother could not always leave at home.
But that beginning was wiped out in fear
The day I swung suspended with the grapes,
And was come after like Eurydice
And brought down safely from the upper regions;
And the life I live now's an extra life
I can waste as I please on whom I please.
So if you see me celebrate two birthdays,
And give myself out of two different ages,
One of them five years younger than I look—

One day my brother led me to a glade
Where a white birch he knew of stood alone,
Wearing a thin head-dress of pointed leaves,
And heavy on her heavy hair behind,
Against her neck, an ornament of grapes.
Grapes, I knew grapes from having seen them last year.
One bunch of them, and there began to be
Bunches all round me growing in white birches,
The way they grew round Leif the Lucky's German;
Mostly as much beyond my lifted hands, though,
As the moon used to seem when I was younger,
And only freely to be had for climbing.
My brother did the climbing; and at first
Threw me down grapes to miss and scatter

And have to hunt for in sweet fern and hardhack;
Which gave him some time to himself to eat,
But not so much, perhaps, as a boy needed.
So then, to make me wholly self-supporting,
He climbed still higher and bent the tree to earth
And put it in my hands to pick my own grapes.
"Here, take a tree-top, I'll get down another.
Hold on with all your might when I let go."
I said I had the tree. It wasn't true.
The opposite was true. The tree had me.
The minute it was left with me alone
It caught me up as if I were the fish
And it the fishpole. So I was translated
To loud cries from my brother of "Let go!
Don't you know anything, you girl? Let go!"
But I, with something of the baby grip
Acquired ancestrally in just such trees
When wilder mothers than our wildest now
Hung babies out on branches by the hands
To dry or wash or tan, I don't know which,
(You'll have to ask an evolutionist)—
I held on uncomplainingly for life.
My brother tried to make me laugh to help me.
"What are you doing up there in those grapes?
Don't be afraid. A few of them won't hurt you.
I mean, they won't pick you if you don't them."
Much danger of my picking anything!
By that time I was pretty well reduced
To a philosophy of hang-and-let-hang.
"Now you know how it feels," my brother said,
"To be a bunch of fox-grapes, as they call them,
That when it thinks it has escaped the fox
By growing where it shouldn't—on a birch,
Where a fox wouldn't think to look for it—
And if he looked and found it, couldn't reach it—
Just then come you and I to gather it.
Only you have the advantage of the grapes

In one way: you have one more stem to cling by,
And promise more resistance to the picker."

One by one I lost off my hat and shoes,
And still I clung. I let my head fall back,
And shut my eyes against the sun, my ears
Against my brother's nonsense; "Drop," he said,
"I'll catch you in my arms. It isn't far."
(Stated in lengths of him it might not be.)
"Drop or I'll shake the tree and shake you down."
Grim silence on my part as I sank lower,
My small wrists stretching till they showed the banjo strings.
"Why, if she isn't serious about it!
Hold tight awhile till I think what to do.
I'll bend the tree down and let you down by it."
I don't know much about the letting down;
But once I felt ground with my stocking feet
And the world came revolving back to me,
I know I looked long at my curled-up fingers,
Before I straightened them and brushed the bark off.
My brother said: "Don't you weigh anything?
Try to weigh something next time, so you won't
Be run off with by birch trees into space."
It wasn't my not weighing anything
So much as my not knowing anything—
My brother had been nearer right before.
I had not taken the first step in knowledge;
I had not learned to let go with the hands,
As still I have not learned to with the heart,
And have no wish to with the heart—nor need,
That I can see. The mind—is not the heart.
I may yet live, as I know others live,
To wish in vain to let go with the mind—
Of cares, at night, to sleep; but nothing tells me
That I need learn to let go with the heart.

Jody Gladding

                                    my ski
                    fox   deer
                                    tracks
line   is   theis   ascaross   of   inquiry

          hingell   snow

                                                              we're trying
              ofolding   to ask
                          into another
                                                        where

          landscape

                                              tree
                                              line
                                                    opens

Jody Gladding

the wind
love is a necessary

                                        relentless

                            sound of **myth**   the perfect
                                storm   O
            there's   torn leaves
        no   twisted
            denying   **it**   free
                        against   **makes things**
                        our   **happen**
                        skin

Louise Glück (Vermont Poet Laureate, 1994-1998)

The Couple in the Park

A man walks alone in the park and beside him a woman walks, also
alone. How does one know? It is as though a line exists between
them, like a line on a playing field. And yet, in a photograph they
might appear a married couple, weary of each other and of the
many winters they have endured together. At another time, they
might be strangers about to meet by accident. She drops her book;
stooping to pick it up, she touches, by accident, his hand and her
heart springs open like a child's music box. And out of the box comes
a little ballerina made of wood. I have created this, the man thinks;
though she can only whirl in place, still she is a dancer of some kind,
not simply a block of wood. This must explain the puzzling music
coming from the trees.

Louise Glück

Burning Leaves

The fire burns up into the clear sky,
eager and furious, like an animal trying to get free,
to run wild as nature intended—
When it burns like this,
leaves aren't enough—it's
acquisitive, rapacious,
refusing to be contained, to accept limits—
There's a pile of stones around it.
Past the stones, the earth's raked clean, bare—
Finally the leaves are gone, the fuel's gone,
the last flames burn upwards and sidewards—
Concentric rings of stones and gray earth
circle a few sparks;
the farmer stomps on these with his boots.
It's impossible to believe this will work—
not with a fire like this, those last sparks
still resisting, unfinished,
believing they will get everything in the end
since it is obvious they are not defeated,
merely dormant or resting, though no one knows
whether they represent life or death.

Louise Glück

Bats

There are two kinds of vision:
the seeing of things, which belongs
to the science of optics, versus
the seeing beyond things, which
results from deprivation. Man mocking the dark, rejecting
worlds you do not know: though the dark
is full of obstacles, it is possible to have
intense awareness when the field is narrow
and the signals few. Night has bred in us
thought more focused than yours, if rudimentary:
man the ego, man imprisoned in the eye,
there is a path you cannot see, beyond the eye's reach,
what the philosophers have called
the *via negativa*: to make a place for light
the mystic shuts his eyes—illumination
of the kind he seeks destroys
creatures who depend on things.

Louise Glück

THE MUSE OF HAPPINESS

The windows shut, the sun rising.
Sounds of a few birds;
the garden filmed with a light moisture.
And the insecurity of great hope
suddenly gone.
And the heart still alert.
And a thousand small hopes stirring,
not new but newly acknowledged.
Affection, dinner with friends.
And the structure of certain
adult tasks.
The house clean, silent.
The trash not needing to be taken out.
It is a kingdom, not an act of imagination:
and still very early,
the white buds of the penstemon open.
Is it possible we have finally paid
bitterly enough?
That sacrifice is not to be required,
that anxiety and terror have been judged sufficient?
A squirrel racing along the telephone wire,
a crust of bread in its mouth.
And darkness delayed by the season.
So that it seems
part of a great gift
not to be feared any longer.
The day unfurling, but very gradually, a solitude
not to be feared, the changes—
faint, barely perceived—
the penstemon open.
The likelihood
of seeing it through to the end.

Barry Goldensohn

THE SUMMER I SPENT SCREWING IN THE BACK SEATS OF STATION WAGONS

was the last summer that lasted all summer.
This was not—do not misread the title—
screwing the seats in, but climbing in
the back seats and screwing as fast as I could.
It was always the same, open the back and fling
in the power driver and the big tool
box with the braces and screws as the tall Pole
pressed the window firmly into place,
as I would drill the holes, line up the clamps,
and screw them in. If the clamps sat too tight
the window cracked and then a flurry of work
as we swarmed ahead of our spot on the line,
the tall Pole and I at Fisher Bodies
in Euclid, Ohio, and rushed to return to our place.
I kept bashing my hands and my nights were crushed,
and in all that soul exhausting work
the cars were as rotten as we could make them.
There was nothing of ourselves we wanted to see
in what we did to Chevy Kingswood and Nomad
and Pontiac Safari with pubescent tailfins.
This was in Euclid, who looked on Beauty bare,
Ohio, whose three long syllables danced
in only four letters, pronounced Ah-hah,
by my fellow workers who wrenched, torqued, and screwed
on the assembly line with me in Euclid, Ohio.
At the end of the day all we had was numbers,
corporate totals. It brought to mind
the boast of Wilt the Stilt that he had fucked
twenty thousand women in his time,
and never, never, the same woman twice.
And as we looked, wearied, at our line of cars
we wondered, how could he tell?

Barry Goldensohn

Old Home Day

Some rode in from farms at the edge of town
or flew in from work in the South and West
to gather around the Common, and the kids
lay down their frisbees for the cloud parade
of life as it's always been with nothing to change—
volunteer firemen and ambulance brigade,
the town cop, vets of foreign wars,
some recent ones that snared the world
with bombs, drones, mortars, BARs.
The wars against their own lead the parade,
vets of the Revolution and Civil War, Texas
against Cheyenne, King Philip's War,
with their flintlocks, muskets, sabers, arrows, bows,
and the band played and the beer flowed like blood,
in this sweet town where everyone knows
everyone's public name and secret name
and all their dead and no one locks their doors.
No one stands aside to see. All join
this unbounded democracy.
Two brothers dead in one campaign
mosey over, AWOL as usual, for beer
and to read their names on the brass plaque again
fixed to an obelisk in the square.

Karin Gottshall

MORE LIES

Sometimes I say I'm going to meet my sister at the café—
even though I have no sister—just because it's such
a beautiful thing to say. I've always thought so, ever since

I read a novel in which two sisters were constantly meeting
in cafés. Today, for example, I walked alone
on the wet sidewalk, wearing my rain boots, expecting

someone might ask where I was headed. I bought
a steno pad and a watch battery, the store windows
fogged up. Rain in April is a kind of promise, and it costs

nothing. I carried a bag of books to the café and ordered
tea. I like a place that's lit by lamps. I like a place
where you can hear people talk about small things,

like the difference between azure and cerulean,
and the price of tulips. It's going down. I watched
someone who could be my sister walk in, shaking the rain

from her hair. I thought, even now florists are filling
their coolers with tulips, five dollars a bundle. All over
the city there are sisters. Any one of them could be mine.

Karin Gottshall

LISTENING TO THE DEAD

I've come unstitched, says the rabbit in the orchard, belly
torn open by dogs. *Maggots have come to sew me back*

into earth. All around, the softening apples
drop when the wind blows and at night deer approach
and lower their slender necks to eat.

I've lost my eyes, says the rabbit,
whose long strong legs lie crossed like a woman's. *But I hear
leaves rustle, and the sound of lifting wings.*

Now the first snow has fallen.
The rabbit says *I can't feel the cold, and something
has chewed away the pads of my paws.*

The clear, dark air is filled with radio signals
from Finland and Peru, voices borne

as far as the empty moon. *Oh, I'm gone*, says the rabbit,
*no lungs, no nose to sniff at the soil's rich iron,
no coat in the rising sun's gold, nor terror, nor tongue.*

Rachel Hadas

A Poultice

Turmeric, rosemary: blend with rum.
Winter is fading, spring will come,

snow will melt, and leaves set in.
Rosemary, turmeric: shake in gin.

Turmeric, bourbon, rosemary:
a blue-green bruise leaks toward my eye

(a week ago I bumped my head).
I swab and bathe it. The bruise will fade

faster with this concoction
recommended by my son.

Soak a cloth and wipe the place.
Weapons are poised to fight in space.

Refugees packed in lifeboats drown.
Cyber attacks: the system's down,

an outage no one can repair.
The turmeric has stained my hair.

The pillow smells of alcohol.
Wind and rain and petals fall.

Sunday excursion: Hamilton Grange,
the empty streets subdued and strange,

the widowed house perched in its park.
White petals gleam in the gathering dark.

April this year is cool and slow.
The stain seeps toward my left eyebrow.

Care for the hurt place: soak, swab, wrap.
And then, before I take a nap,

dab the spot with oil of myrrh.
The poultice: patience and desire.

Turmeric, rosemary, and rum:
My love and I are rocked in time.

The motion lulls us, we forget
the bruise, the wound, the doom, the threat.

Rachel Hadas

The Golden Road

On a September road, I met my son
walking the other way. I had the hill
to climb; he was returning from a run.
　　No surprises; he
　　knew I was nearby,
as I knew he was. But precisely where
our paths might meet was a benign surprise.

The road was rutted, plastered with gold leaf.
Did our eyes, as we neared each other, meet?
More of a full-body recognition:
　　this tall young stranger
　　striding silently
around a bend, who paused on seeing me
(however I appeared) and then passed on.

Autumnal radiance thickened
by complications, memory, history –
nothing startling, in my mother's phrase.
　　The gold road curves.
　　The living pass the dead.
Old and young acknowledge one another;
then each takes their separate path ahead.

Oh Muse, peel off your dove-gray cardigan.
September, fallen leaves, and cool noon sun:
I rounded a gold curve and saw my son.

Walter Hard

In War Time

The mellow wind bent the grass making a light green wave
That billowed along the hill toward the brook.
Under an elm black and white cows stood.
Birds flew here and there.
Their songs made ripples in the flowing rustle of the leaves.
Across the valley there was a farmhouse,
And a grey barn and a leaning silo.
Bush-covered stone walls hid the road
That climbed the hill slantwise to get a better footing.
There was a row of maples near the farmhouse--
Fulfilled promises made to some thoughtful forebear,
Long since done with promises and planting.
Meadows, pastures, plowed land with brush division lines;
And cloud shadows drifting over the precise patterns,
Paying no heed to fences or earth's ideas of order.
Up the slope the grey shadows crept
To fade against the green wall of mountain.
All the sounds were gentle,
Each fitting in to make silence into sound
without robbing silence.
The smooth pastures curved to the green hills
Which took them to the mothering serenity of the mountain.
Peace lured the soul.
How to be a part of this tranquil pattern,
How to hold forever this elemental peace,
And still not be a tree or grass or four-footed beast!

Walter Hard

The Kelly Stand

Memories of the old days
Are often memories of a life that was hard.
The labors of pioneers to clear the forest;
The struggles to wrest a living from the soil;
The isolation of mountain farms.
But the old tavern is holding fast to the gay days.
Perhaps its walls are weather beaten and bulging,
And its piazza roof hangs down like a closed eyelid,
And its floors are rotting.
It's true that bricks strew the hearth
And its staircase is broken and shaky.

But under the sagging roof
The ballroom still stands,
With its arched ceiling clean and white.
The cracks in the plaster
Are only the wrinkles of old age.
The floor still springs as it used to do
When dancing feet made merry.

There, around the wall, are the built-in benches,
Where the tired dancers rested,
After the final mad whirl of the Tempest.
There is the musicians' stand,
With the long music rack across the front,
Where the four fiddlers drew their bows
Stirring the blood of many a girl and swain.

Listen! Can't you hear the prompter's call
Above the shuffle of the rhythmic step
And the mad surge of the singing fiddles?

Perhaps there by the wide fan window
You may see two lovers

Gazing off at the mountains
Mountains, tall, silent, enchanted,
In the summer moonlight.

A rotting shell, the Old Tavern,
Full of ruin and decay,
While the carefree dancing steps
Still echo through the arched ballroom.
They're dancing to the eerie music of the wind
In the tall dark spruces
By the wide fan window.

Pamela Harrison

So, Caravaggio

The table is cleared
and I am waiting
for what comes.
Cup and plate,
fork and spoon,
one by one
you have removed
every last legacy,
every tarnished ideal
until there is nothing
but bare wood
and my clasped hands.
I will sit at the table
and open my ears
to the silence,
get comfortable
with it, as its guest, until
this emptiness overflows.
A light hangs low
over the table,
centering the room.
All that's inessential
falls from view. For now,
just silence,
the bare table, my ready hands,
a narrow arc of light,
the bounding dark.

Pamela Harrison

FIELD IN SNOW

I stand at the window watching snow fall
on the meadow, bending the barbed canes
of bramble, dried clusters of chokecherry
disdained by birds, the twisted crabapple
caught in wild grape coils. Bleached and buried,

the sway of empty field marks the passing
of an understanding that sustained me
like the very ground. At the point of entering
this ending, of opening to the nothingness
that surrounds, I am afraid. I know how snow falls,

how impersonally it fills the hollows of a field,
how painlessly it passes into water in the spring
or rises warming into mist above the cooler ground.
I am afraid because I understand the worth
of what I leave behind

because it has, like the days and all they contain,
flowed into me, become a part of me,
so that, stepping out now into the whiteness,
into the softly falling, imperturbable snow,
I know only, feel only, the dying of what I was.

Nothing I could name could replace this dying,
nothing beyond the opening, a winter field
in which possibility might one day move
like the deer I sometimes see at dawn,
shadows stepping into darker trees.

Geof Hewitt

Toilet Knuckles

That's what the kids called bagels, *toilet knuckles.*
Brothers. Brothers with a language
built on inflection and direct metaphor,
none of this waffling typical of similes.

Brothers that hunt together and when they sing
without rehearsal their voices blend and the tone is true.
No gimmicks except that secret language
of the almost imperceptibly curled lip

or a double beat of the eyelids only the other
feels, and note how I didn't say sees or notices.
We are outsiders in the deepest sense
made deeper by our jealousy.

Geof Hewitt

Wrestling To Lose

None of us were winners, like
Armentrout or Beebe, the heavyweight
who surprised opponents twice his size
in the Unlimited Division, flipping one
who still scowled from the peevish handshake
that had to start each match.

Spring Weekend my parents drove my date up from New Jersey
and I wrestled the 135 pounder from Peddie
who took 30 seconds to pin me Spring Weekend
the year before. My father
clapped my back in the locker room
and pronounced it "a moral victory."

Behind the gym two weeks later
the hacks on the team smoked their first cigarettes
since fall and chafed at the gung hoes
who were still running laps. Where are they now?
Well, Armentrout's big in business for sure,
and Beebe's a famous neurosurgeon!

And us hackers? I'll hazard our wages
per capita can't touch *theirs*. We were artists,
idealists, the boys who invented wrestling to lose:
slam yourself down on the mat. With shoulders flat
hold your opponent just three seconds over you
helpless in the victory pose.

Tamra J. Higgins

My Father's Birth, Iowa, 1932

While a late March blizzard clogged all thoughts
of spring and any up-coming, well-rooted life,
a doctor labored on foot through the last few
miles to reach the farmhouse, cut off
by the raging white. Within minutes
of his arrival he set aside a two-pound baby boy
at the foot of the bed, like an extra pillow in the way,
covered him with a corner of the sheet then turned
back to the mother, nearly dead.
Why tend to flotsam floating free,
three months earlier than it should have been.
In kerosene shadows he watched and washed the woman,
rolled her over to place towels on the blood-soaked bed,
his raw fingers on her ghost-white hip.
He wondered *could she have had a hand in this?*
If one of them survived, let it be
the mother; she had two boys already, and these farmers,
the doctor knew, scraped like hens to eat.

A cricket's chirp meant nothing in that wind-
battered shack, though in winter it became
a curious endurance. The doctor's focus
almost made him miss a second chirp of insect-song,
but the strange note caught him in a pause; and he raised
his head from the woman's moans, took a step
to inspect the newborn, still bare, still cold,
still where it was cast. Perhaps, the doctor thought,
he should help it after all, though if it survived what
would come of it? What becomes of a speck
of dust in the corner of the universe?

He called for the father who appeared, shadows
under his cheek-bones, a few teeth gone,
the toddlers in his arms. "Fetch me someone

to help." A farm hand, Clem, fired up the stove again,
heated the kettle of water and brought in a bushel basket
from the shed. The doctor bundled the baby,
who started kicking in the warmth, settled
him in a shoe-box and the shoe-box in the basket.
Clem filled up mason-jars with the heated water,
wedged them into the basket, around that chirping bird.
Night came on.

In the morning, an uncle and a grandfather
arrived. The mother, eyes still closed, gave
a nod, so the men got the wagon ready, hitched
up the horses who were fighting against
the snow just to leave the barn. The doctor
didn't let on what he thought of the endeavor
when they piled the blankets on the home-made
incubator. The men whisked the basket
to the wagon, pulled the horse the first
few feet to show that they weren't joking.

They headed towards the hospital in town.
What lengths these foolish men were taking!
Why risk so much? The baby probably wouldn't
make it. And if he did survive, what would
he become? At most, another mouth they
couldn't feed, another boy who bled.

Tamra J. Higgins

This is Water

This is about a lake that opened up one night
in the night a man—who knows the reason why—
why, he may have been drunk, or maybe he was drunk
on love. His love involved water that night, that night—
I was only a teenager home for once on a summer night;
we were all home: a strange confluence of paths that brought
us all together that summer. It was hot and the lake was there
lying at the edge of a flat sleeping Iowa town,
and the man was there. A boat was involved.

It was hot. The lake was small. No one could sleep well,
but we did, we did doze in and out of sweaty dreams
though everything else had stopped in the heat: the bugs, the cars,
the breeze. Nothing could move except a word that rose
from the water: help.

By the time the word had drifted in the air that hung like a man
on a raft, hung until the next help pushed it off the surface of the water
nudged it onto the land into my bedroom window into my dream

by the time I made it to the front porch and found my sister,
one of my brothers already sitting on the cement steps,
the steps cool in the night as I sat next to them by the time
I sat on the porch with my back against a pillar while more voices rose
in the dark and lights appeared on the lake as though the voices

themselves were the source of the light; the light sweeping and slicing
the water, voices sweeping and slicing the darkness, a voice, a light,
a voice, a light, then darkness, silence, water

.

David Huddle

What Can You Tell Me About Your Father?

Around people he was rarely at ease
but when he could settle into himself—
reading the *Roanoke Times*, watching TV,
or paying bills—he seemed comfortable.
I studied him when we had company.
He had nice manners, asked polite questions,
tried not to talk about himself—I think he
feared being the center of attention.
What he liked best was when mother's Uncle
Bo came to our house to play chess with him.
Reticent as a tree and deeply humble,
that man and my father played their slow games
saying almost nothing. Did they have fun?
I can't say. But those games went on and on.

David Huddle

WOULD YOU REPEAT THE QUESTION PLEASE?

for Jane Ambrose

Pew after pew of us gray-haired mourners
our smiles those of living ghosts acting like
Jane's dead but she's here somewhere of course
we can't see her but she's sort of alive....
From way back death's been our moody girlfriend
scrunched up against the passenger-side door
won't talk won't smile just smokes & pouts she'd end
the relationship if we'd just stop the car
but lately she's gotten friendlier this
past year she put her hand on my thigh her tongue
in my ear O Jane why did you say yes
to that cunning bitch remember how once
we were children sitting at desks in school
with you our droll girl liveliest of us all?

Cynthia Huntington

UNTITLED

Before there was light there was wind and it rained on the newborn earth
four million years. The cloud vapor was so thick no sunlight reached the
earth. We were burning, even the rain could not cool us. On ourselves we
rained, in one self we burned—our self was all one mass and all we are
was present then, already understood. There could be no thought yet of
continents or seas, no forest, fern, or bog, nothing living and nothing to
live upon. But everything was. Molten rock, that great creation soup,
simmered, bubbled—take and eat. It was my body. There is a planet that
is a diamond. It lies near to us in our own galaxy, this Milky Way, Path of
Ghosts, the stepping stones that spirits follow through the spiral out
onto the other edge, the nothing before being. This diamond planet laid
along their way rings like a gong in space, it chimes an aching high note;
they must not stop there but continue on, the lonely, last, difficult,
desired leaving that is return, and it is said they begin to remember as
they approach, to long for what they came out from, stars and darkness.
Then they are glad. Not they, but us. We are those spirits finding our way
without eyes. Before there was light there was wind and it was a new
earth. And before this earth, there was no wind, we could not rain on
ourselves, we had not begun, and, unfallen, we knew no path to rise.

Cynthia Huntington

GENOME

Once we were one.
Then wandered, set feet forth
ahead and onward gone;
apart to walk, small bands to roam.
Northing to wind, and wending went
along rough ways. No path or road
then; there we were
wind without end, all scattered,
broken up, undone.

Once we were one. Like wind we bore,
were borne, were outward flung.
Sound waves from single drum.
In one time only, one, no time to come
until we break and go
out from this place away
into a land of dust and stars.
I show you kin,
clan, cousin, tribe: we wandered far,
we strayed to turn
life opening called beyond.

Now take him wife from neighbor's tent,
be onward gone.
Girl given stranger suffer mother's grief.
Break ties to bind, make new.
We must have lost to find,
to come upon, to know.
Be broken to know other, second, else,
in whom we find the other who is not
the self, toward whom the self
may bend. These strangers who
are not ourselves in whom
we find the lost again.

Major Jackson

Double View of the Adirondacks as Reflected Over Lake Champlain from Waterfront Park

The mountains are at their theater again,
each ridge practicing an oration of scale and crest,
and the sails, performing glides across the lake, complain
for being out-shadowed despite their gracious
bows. Thirteen years in this state, what hasn't occurred?
A cyclone in my spirit led to divorce, four books
gave darkness an echo of control, my slurred
hand finding steadiness by the prop of a page,
and God, my children whom I scarred! Pray they forgive.
My crimes felt mountainous, yet perspective
came with distance, and like those peaks, once keening
beneath biting ice, then felt resurrection in a vestige
of water, unfrozen, cascading and adding to the lake's
depth, such have I come to gauge my own screaming.
The masts tip so far they appear to capsize, keeling
over where every father is a boat on water. The wakes
carry the memory of battles, and the Adirondacks
hold their measure. I am a tributary of something greater.

Major Jackson

ENCHANTERS OF ADDISON COUNTY

We were more than gestural, close-listening,
the scent of manure writing its waft on the leaves
off Route 22A. By nightfall, our gaze flecked
like loon cries, but no one was up for turnips
nor other roots, not least of which the clergy.
Romanticism has its detractors, which is why
we lined the road with tea-lit luminaries
and fresh-cut lemons. We called it making magic,
then stormed the corners and porches
of General Stores, kissing whenever cars idled
at four way stop signs or sought Grade A maple syrup
in tin containers with painted scenes of horse-drawn
farmers plowing through snow. The silhouetted, rusted
farm equipment gave us the laidback heaven
we so often wished, and fireflies bequeathed earth stars,
such blink and blank and bunk-a-bunk-bunk.
And of course we wondered if we existed,
and also too, the cows of the ancient pastures,
and the white milk inside our heads
like church spires and ice cream cones.
Even after all of that cha-cha-cha, we still came
out of swimming holes shivering our hearts out.

Reuben Jackson

My Mother in the Afterlife

It is 1970 again.
My Mother is shaking her head
At the sight of my clothing.

She never abandoned her dream
Of a world without denim—

Now there's no escaping her critique.

("You can't have coffee with God
looking like that!")

She rolls her eyes at Abbie Hoffman—
And at Bill—
Who owned the head shop
Near our house.

Death has restored her mind.
Now she's talking curfew.

My brother laughs behind a cloud.

Reuben Jackson

A DAY IN THE LIFE
(BLACK IN VERMONT MIX)

You're a nigger.

A public radio
Treasure.

A public radio
Nigger treasure.

10:00 AM—
A neighbor smiles
In the elevator.

10:05—
The man behind the
counter calls the cops.

Phyllis Katz

LETTER TO MYSELF

Forget your fear your memory
is going, thought as crooked
as your arthritic fingers, difficult
to flex as well, aging molecules
in a brain unable to recall parts of your past.
Forget that this morning you could not
summon *Eggs Benedict* at breakfast
however much your tried.

Find comfort in involuntary triggers –
those luscious Proustian madeleines,
uninvited guests arriving in the empty
chambers of your mind: pungent smell
of horse sweat, softness of a baby's head,
taps at sunset, taste of mountain blueberries,
flute song of the Hermit Thrush, sudden
wind puffs ruffling a sleeping lake.

Phyllis Katz

CURRICULUM VITAE AT SEVENTY-FOUR

Did I dream when we were young
and full of hope, we'd always dance all night,
work all day without a sign of weariness?

Our yesterdays have vanished
as quickly as the breath of summer
I felt this morning brush my lips as I awoke.

What we have done in all our years
is printed on pages
soon forgotten like dusty books
aging on shelves that no one ever visits.

But in early dew to have traced the tracks
of the fox's journey through the meadow,
pattern of turkeys' passage in the snow,
to have seen at night a shower of Perseids,

to have watched the glow of Northern lights,
have sat beneath the reddening maple tree
beside the pond listening to the silence
of leaves floating on its surface,

to have watched the growing
of our children's children,
and to have held each other through the times of
pain and darkness

will have been enough.

Galway Kinnell (Vermont Poet Laureate, 1989-1993)

VAPOR TRAIL REFLECTED IN THE FROG POND

1

The old watch: their
thick eyes
puff and foreclose by the moon. The young, heads
trailed by the beginnings of necks,
shiver,
in the guarantee they shall be bodies.

In the frog pond
the vapor trail of a SAC bomber creeps,

I hear its drone, drifting, high up
in immaculate ozone.

2

And I hear,
coming over the hills, America singing,
her varied carols I hear:
crack of deputies' rifles practicing their aim on stray dogs at night,
sput of cattleprod,
TV going on about the smells of the human body,
curses of the soldier as he poisons, burns, grinds, and stabs
the rice of the world,
with open mouth, crying strong, hysterical curses.

3

And by paddies in Asia
bones
wearing a few shadows
walk down a dirt road, smashed
bloodsuckers on their heel, knowing
flesh thrown down in the sunshine
dogs shall eat
and flesh flung into the air

shall be seized by birds,
shoulder blades smooth, unmarked by old feather-holes,
hands rivered
by blue, erratic wanderings of the blood,
eyes crinkled shut at almost seeing
the drifting sun that gives us our lives.

Galway Kinnell

Fergus Falling

He climbed to the top
of one of those million white pines
set out across the emptying pastures
of the fifties—some program to enrich the rich
and rebuke the forefathers
who cleared it all at once with ox and axe—
climbed to the top, probably to get out
of the shadow
not of those forefathers but of this father,
and saw for the first time,
down in its valley, Bruce Pond, giving off
its little steam in the afternoon,

pond where Clarence Akley came on Sunday mornings to cut down the cedars
    around the shore, I'd sometimes hear the slow spondees of his work,
    he's gone,
where Milton Norway came up behind me while I was fishing and stood awhile
    before I knew he was there, he's the one who put the cedar shingles on the
    house, some have curled or split, a few have blown off, he's gone,
where Gus Newland logged in the cold snap of '58, the only man willing to go
    into those woods that never got warmer than ten below, he's gone,
pond where two wards of the state wandered on Halloween, the National
    Guard searched for them in November, in vain, the next fall a hunter
    found their skeletons huddled together, in vain, they're gone,
pond where an old fisherman in a rowboat sits, drowning hooked worms,
    when he goes he's replaced and is never gone,

and when Fergus
saw the pond for the first time
in the clear evening, saw its oldness down there
in its old place in the valley, he became heavier suddenly
in his bones
the way fledglings do just before they fly,
and the soft pine cracked…

I would not have heard his cry
if my electric saw had been working,
its carbide teeth speeding through the bland spruce of our time,
    or scorching
black arcs into some scavenged hemlock plank,
like dark circles under eyes
when the brain thinks too close to the skin,
but I was sawing by hand, and I heard that cry
as though he were attacked; we ran out,
when we bent over him he said, "Galway, Inés, I saw a pond!"
His face went gray, his eyes fluttered closed a frightening moment.

Yes—a pond
that lets off its mist
on clear afternoons of August, in that valley
to which many have come, for their reasons,
from which many have gone, a few for their reasons, most not,
where even now an old fisherman only the pinetops can see
sits in the dry gray wood of his rowboat, waiting for pickerel.

Galway Kinnell

LITTLE SLEEP'S-HEAD SPROUTING HAIR IN THE MOONLIGHT

1

You cry, waking from a nightmare.

When I sleepwalk
into your room, and pick you up,
and hold you up in the moonlight, you cling to me
hard,
as if clinging could save us. I think
you think
I will never die, I think I exude
to you the permanence of smoke or stars,
even as
my broken arms heal themselves around you.

2

I have heard you tell
the sun, *don't go down,* I have stood by
as you told the flower, *don't grow old,*
don't die. Little Maud,

I would blow the flame out of your silver cup,
I would suck the rot from your fingernail,
I would brush your sprouting hair of the dying light,
I would scrape the rust off your ivory bones,
I would help death escape through the little ribs of your body,
I would alchemize the ashes of your cradle back into wood,
I would let nothing of you go, ever,

until washerwomen
feel the clothes fall asleep in their hands,
and hens scratch their spell across hatchet blades,
and rats walk away from the culture of the plague,
and iron twists weapons toward the true north,

and grease refuses to slide in the machinery of progress,
and men feel as free on earth as fleas on the bodies of men,
and lovers no longer whisper to the presence beside them in the dark,
   O corpse-to-be...

And yet perhaps this is the reason you cry,
this the nightmare you wake screaming from:
being forever
in the pre-trembling of a house that falls.

            3
In a restaurant once, everyone
quietly eating, you clambered up
on my lap: to all
the mouthfuls rising toward
all the mouths, at the top of your voice
you cried
your one word, *caca! caca! caca!*
and each spoonful
stopped, a moment, in midair, in its withering
steam.

Yes,
you cling because
I, like you, only sooner
than you, will go down
the path of vanished alphabets,
the roadlessness
to the other side of the darkness,
your arms
like the shoes left behind,
like the adjectives
in the halting speech of old folks,
which once could call up the lost nouns.

4

And you yourself,
some impossible Tuesday
in the year Two Thousand and Nine, will walk out
among the black stones
of the field, in the rain,

and the stones saying
over their one word, *ci-gît, ci-gît, ci-gît,*

and the raindrops
hitting you on the fontanel
over and over, and you standing there
unable to let them in.

5

If one day it happens
you find yourself with someone you love
in a café at one end
of the Pont Mirabeau, at the zinc bar
where wine finds its shapes in upward opening glasses,

and if you commit then, as we did, the error
of thinking,
one day all this will only be memory,

learn to reach deeper
into the sorrows
to come—to touch
the almost imaginary bones
under the face, to hear under the laughter
the wind crying across the black stones. Kiss
the mouth
that tells you, *here,*
here is the world. This mouth. This laughter. These temple bones.

The still undanced cadence of vanishing.

6

In the light the moon
sends back, I can see in your eyes
the hand that waved once
in my father's eyes, a tiny kite
wobbling far up in the twilight of his last look:

and the angel
of all mortal things lets go the string.

7

Back you go, into your crib.

The last blackbird lights up his gold wings: *farewell.*
Your eyes close inside your head,
in sleep. Already
in your dreams the hours begin to sing.

Little sleep's-head sprouting hair in the moonlight,
when I come back
we will go out together,
we will walk out together among
the ten thousand things,
each scratched in time with such knowledge, *the wages
of dying is love.*

Galway Kinnell

THE BEAR

1

In late winter
I sometimes glimpse bits of steam
coming up from
some fault in the old snow
and bend close and see it is lung-colored
and put down my nose
and know
the chilly, enduring odor of bear.

2

I take a wolf's rib and whittle
it sharp at both ends
and coil it up
and freeze it in blubber and place it out
on the fairway of the bears.

And when it has vanished
I move out on the bear tracks,
roaming in circles
until I come to the first, tentative, dark
splash on the earth.

And I set out
running, following the splashes
of blood wandering over the world.
At the cut, gashed resting places
I stop and rest,
at the crawl-marks
where he lay out on his belly
to overpass some stretch of bauchy ice
I lie out
dragging myself forward with bear-knives in my fists.

3
On the third day I begin to starve,
at nightfall I bend down as I knew I would
at a turd sopped in blood,
and hesitate, and pick it up,
and thrust it in my mouth, and gnash it down,
and rise
and go on running.

4
On the seventh day,
living by now on bear blood alone,
I can see his upturned carcass far out ahead, a scraggled,
steamy hulk,
the heavy fur riffling in the wind.

I come up to him
and stare at the narrow-spaced, petty eyes,
the dismayed
face laid back on the shoulder, the nostrils
flared, catching
perhaps the first taint of me as he
died.

I hack
a ravine in his thigh, and eat and drink,
and tear him down his whole length
and open him and climb in
and close him up after me, against the wind,
and sleep.

5
And dream
of lumbering flatfooted
over the tundra,
stabbed twice from within,

splattering a trail behind me,
splattering it out no matter which way I lurch,
no matter which parabola of bear-transcendence,
which dance of solitude I attempt,
which gravity-clutched leap,
which trudge, which groan.

6

Until one day I totter and fall—
fall on this
stomach that has tried so hard to keep up,
to digest the blood as it leaked in,
to break up
and digest the bone itself: and now the breeze
blows over me, blows off
the hideous belches of ill-digested bear blood
and rotted stomach
and the ordinary, wretched odor of bear,

blows across
my sore, lolled tongue a song
or screech, until I think I must rise up
and dance. And I lie still.

7

I awaken I think. Marshlights
reappear, geese
come trailing again up the flyway.
In her ravine under old snow the dam-bear
lies, licking
lumps of smeared fur
and drizzly eyes into shapes
with her tongue. And one
hairy-soled trudge stuck out before me,
the next groaned out,
the next,

the next,
the rest of my days I spend
wandering: wondering
what, anyway,
was that sticky infusion, that rank flavor of blood, that poetry, by
which I lived?

Leland Kinsey

Fish Eggs

So you fished each of the Three Forks,
rediscovering The Corps' discovery.
I wish I could cover those waters with you.
Yes, I went to Labrador again,
fished the upper reaches of the Atikonak
for brook trout, *grande rouges* they call them,
and ouananiche. My arms ached
one day from catching and releasing.
I landed one towards day's end
in a long fast riffle, as others swam
upstream, backs out of the water,
between my legs and all around.
I slipped the two long sets of eggs
out of the belly of the big red,
and set them on a rock.
The eggs had the color and look
of the drupelets of cloudberries
I'd gathered in my creel
at the edges of string bogs.
The eggs and berries were to be my gift
to the Inuit woman
who cooked my evening meals.
I turned to wash the spine blood
from my catch, half a minute,
and when I turned back, a gull sat
where the eggs had been,
a slight gel coating beneath its webbed toes.
Eggs, and no gull noticed,
gull, and no eggs to be seen,
no one's rights involved,
just, quick as that,
life's magic
act.

Leland Kinsey

In The Cranberry Bog

The large cranberry plants arch
over the water or close to the run
flowing from beaver dams above
and slowed to a channel
through the sphagnum flats,
which stretch like fields
toward the open water
of the remaining kettle pond.
The peat moss lies purple, orange
over brush-root hummocks
often topped with small cranberries
like carnelian beads,
but they are not the crop I'm after.

Moose paths, vole and lemming runs,
crisscross the sedgy quaking bog,
which often sinks enough beneath me
so the water almost overtops
my tall boots. At the most quivery
places I gingerly sidestep,
not wanting to break through
to whatever muddy soup,
whatever black-water rooms,
the vegetative mat floats above.

The large cranberries often grow thickest
around greyed cedar stumps
that line the dank banks.
I stoop each by each
and the berries come to hand hazy
but are finger brushed
to a deep plum color
as they rattle into my pail.

Dolls eye berries of dogbane
seem to peer over the scene.
Chewed berries and seeds lie
in piles by rodent nest entrances
to small halls in the drier hummocks.

I've knelt picking, looking close,
like this in Labrador,
where each tiny hillock, moss-topped,
through which dew berries push,
is a small tableau in late August
of a New England round mountain
in mid fall. I'm surrounded
by a number of the latter this gathering day,
but, knees wet, hands cold, senses startled,
I focus on the miniature scene,
and feel delight as large
as if the part were the whole,
as if there were a whole.

Adrie Kusserow

Patchwork Quilt for a Congolese Refugee
(*Underhill Center, Vermont*)

None of the white coats
    predicted the autumn leaves would be such a trigger.

Every fall she grows suspicious
    as the days pass, sly and dark, behind her
and the earth shifts slowly in its seat.

Blood orange blotches catch and spread
    like birthmarks along the mountain range.
In the cold, balding woods where they tell her to walk,

she can hardly breathe when she sees it,
    the sugar maples' gory neon spill,
as if kicked in the gut,

the first burning vein,
    scarlet bolt of lightning,

She could spend her whole life
    picking through images
of machete-gutted women,

cobbling together a patchwork quilt of ragged rapes
    with its bold "African" patterns so in vogue now.
She could fall in love, like some have,

with Ted-talking the noble tragedy of her story,
    even deftly sewing the dull needle of Jesus
through the little jungle brute

who crammed a gun up her nose,
	stunning the audience into silence.

She could drag it around like the American kids
	with their baby blankets,
demanding their rights to bedtime stories.

She could even sell it at the boutiques
	where Americans shop for Fair Trade.
Or, as the eerie geese fly south above her

and the cold creeps across her skin,
	crimson gashes ripping through the hills
with their brilliant mad infections,

she could let the blood leaves
	break her apart, let go of it all
and finally just begin.

Adrie Kusserow

LADYSLIPPER, RED EFT

(Underhill Center, Vermont)

As a child I awoke
to the furiousness of bees.

All morning my mother and I combed the woods
for red efts, trout lily, trillium.

I learned young
the smell of God and soil.

The first time I saw a ladyslipper
I felt embarrassed, the pink-veined pouches,

simultaneously ephemeral and genital,
floating toad-balloons,

half scrotum, half fairy,
half birth, half death.

Without the formalities of church and school
lust and spirit first came to me

as one—
through the potent hips of spring.

But flowers, like fear, once inside me
never lay still—

amidst my restless
stalking of the woods,

I wanted something bulky to thank,
to name, to explain all the impossible grace.

So I dragged my thirsty body
over the hills, into the trees.

I let the plump red efts, orange fingers tiny as rain,
crawl across my neck, onto my cheek,

half reptile, half elf,
half earth, half magic.

Years passed,
spring after spring cycled through me,

again and again I arrived in heaven
through touch,

lust, even, for the wrinkled pouches of ladyslipper,
the soft lemon bellied efts

that waddled pigeon-toed across my palm.
Now I walk my daughter through April's black mud.

It's been a long winter,
she hasn't quite unfurled.

Still, she sticks her ear into the cacophony of crows
above us, the way a dog sniffs

at a tight current of scent.
Across the meadow the peepers

gossip in their giant cities,
salamanders toddle

over the black soil,
back into the cold ponds they think of as mother.

awake, awake
what if, what if

What if God is walking through us,
picking seasons, histories, humans off

like milkweed from a sweater,
wading through us,

a slow giant through warm ponds,
feeling the odd tickle of religions

like tangled weeds at his feet.
I watch Ana now in full bloom,

despite the rain, running outside barefoot,
setting up dolls' nests in the fields,

collecting moles, covering them in leaves,
naming them even though they're dead.

She skitters across the garden, singing,
she too is learning young

the restlessness of rapture,
the way beauty is hard to sit with,

the way it bends the body into prayer,
the way ripeness must be touched.

Soft black earth of the garden,
she and her brother all fists and toes.

I watch her digging into heaven—
soil, toads, bulbs, buds,

the craning neck of spring—
and all summer

the sweet long green meadows.

Joan Hutton Landis

ORTOLANS

Your bank gives a whopper
at the Hotel St. George, show stopper,
gorgeous   cut flowers   teased hair....
You shake hands with the Big Man
and his powerful women
lit by their jewels' glare. Sedated
by dry martinis and the curious palliative
care of caviar, cannabis and other délices,
we prepare to endear each to the other,
like lovers; investment first, then all things green.

A waiter appears with a platter
of ortolans, raked on three skewers—
songbirds shot by boys this morning
up in the hills above Beirut,
thrilling the Levs, chilling the real me
who fed nuthatch and chickadee
back in New Jersey, not yet four.
Now take my stiletto
and skewer the lips of two eaters
so the dead birds line up in gullets,
pullet after pullet—until the swallower
chokes. "Stand on your hands
to disgourge the ortolans." In answer
to genuine dred and sobs
I lose my nerve, offer them more
of the killed, grilled, crunchy kabobs.

Joan Hutton Landis

SPECULATION

Thirst is not the worst end I might suffer,
no drop of liquid for relief;
I'd expire with gratitude knowing it was tougher
to die while burning at the stake of false belielf.

Or should my end depend on some dark virus
that cancelled all the workings of my gut,
I'd fill my vases up with purple iris
and golden grapes that Midas willed to Egypt's Tut.

No. Parkinson's Disease will kill me easily,
using only one self-manufactured tool,
hidden like the weeds that choke the small Sargasso Sea—
I study Billy Budd as silent Angel, speaking Fool,
not unaware of how unfair his given destiny,
first choking, then drowning in his own unejaculated drool.

Alexis Lathem

BÉRGÈRE

Ville du Château du Passy, France

1.

At this hour I watch the light gather up the wheat in her blue nets.
The ground thickens with mist and the throat of evening
gurgles and purrs. The goats are in their beds.
I can hear the mice softly thumping beneath the eaves.
I have made my home here,
learning to navigate my troupe of goats
past blue wheat and fields of seedlings,
to occupy this granary with its many shadows,
a family of mice and one *hirondelle*.

It's still dark when I go to rouse the troupe,
drive them into the milking room,
where they line up their rumps to me.
I know each of them by the size and feel of their udders,
still warm with sleep, the shape and curve of their backs.
I slip my hands through their hind legs to take their milk
while they munch on grain.
They have accepted this bargain.
This one has deep cuts from barbed wire
across the tender skin of an udder.
When I grip and pull down on her teat
she lets out the scratchy, witch-like bleat
of the dead.

O poet asleep in your granary of words,
waiting for a new moon to be born in a hay bale,
for the smell of dung and must in the straw piles

to waft with frankincense and myrrh,
for the knife to fall from the butcher's hand
and the ram to walk away like Isaac from the block.
For the end to turn back to the beginning
where the dung drops to dust and gives life
to wheat and sunflower,
where a drop of milk clings to a teat like Saturn's last moon,
and the blood in its puddle of afterbirth swirls in its diaphanous sac
and the cow swallows it whole the way the universe drinks its stars.
Leaving you these words in the dusty chink of a windowsill:
Hirondelle. Milk Pail. Bell.

Alexis Lathem

PSALM

When I see the dusty husk of a milkweed
in autumn, I think of him, in his.

In his last days, a milky stain on his lips,
he had the skin of candlewax and the smell

of tin. His voice rattled though there was
no wind. In spring, who will think

of the prickly teasel, the last wizened apples
the deer have left. The azaleas, the magnolias,

will be in bloom, like a hemorrhage.
And the perfumy smell of peonies.

The greenish new skin of the bereaved
makes us look peculiar, like river rocks

that have been all winter under ice.
The light dazzles us. We do not know

what, we do not know what to do
with these bodies, and with this presence

that will be a recurring source
of silence, like the heron who keeps

returning, who stands at the water's edge
as if it were reading a book, and then,

when it lifts its wings, appears to be turning
the page, passing over it like a hand.

How do words mean any more than water does?
I do not know if the wrinkle on the water,

or the cottony tuft of the milkweed flower—
does it want to be remembered, or let go.

In memory of my brother Niles (1955-2007)

DUBBER'S CUR

— for John Engels (1931-2007)

At last one day I used a trick you may have heard of:
I loaded a 12-gauge shell
with rocksalt and shot him from distance enough I'd hurt him plenty
but do no actual harm.
He gave a satisfactory yelp and bolted over
our ridge, blond blur of sinew.

A scary thing to look at, he must be partly pit bull
—the telltale eyes and boxy
countenance—but mixed with something much, much bigger.
He's a brute, all maw and chest.
And yet as far as I can tell there's no mean streak
in Buddy, who's not to blame:

Dubber just can't seem to keep him home. Or won't.
Every morning Buddy
winds our own dogs up, and pees on each last post
and door and flowerstalk.
That day of the shooting, I told myself I'd had enough
this time, and told my family,

"We won't see *him* again." In only a matter of hours
he climbed back up to us
from that junkheap ramble of trailers, pickups, scrap iron, tires,
down where Dubber lives
with his wife by common law and two young roly daughters
still at home, each girl
with at least one child of her own. The Lord knows how they keep
body and soul together.
Some time later—and who can say how a thing can start
to brew in a person's mind? —

while driving back from the upscale market five towns south,
hauling salmon, French bread,

organic greens in our foreign car, I came to think
how likely it was that Buddy
had wandered in once more to lift his leg somewhere.
All our house dogs, meanwhile,
who in fact should daily bark their thanks to God they *are*
just that, house dogs, inside,

not mixing it up with him—our dogs would again be slavering
on the windows, howling at Buddy.
I swore by habit, then somehow felt: *At times your life
can lift you from the factual.*
I was more than glad for that, no matter it came so sudden,
and didn't make any sense,

and doesn't accord with anything a man could prove
or defend, or even want to.
In that same moment, I envisioned my penniless neighbor's mongrel,
his dauntless, tireless Buddy,
trotting his usual beat up the face of that murderous ridge
leaving his wretched gang

to eke out its day, the sun pouring down through a crack in the
mountains
buttery in the vision
on the dog's thick fur, heraldic. And he seemed an admirable creature,
if only for his patience.
More: the house and hovels, the twisted wrecks of chassis
and antique farm machine

all seemed to assume a kindred glow, and so seemed part
of something much, much bigger.
The wetnose kids, the scrabbling barncats, pullets, poults,
the scrawny pony and weedy
garden plot . . . . Forgive me,
but these all testified to a light in each of us,

though don't embarrass me,
don't ask a thing about it. Instead, let me ask *you*:
have you not in your wandering
a world that you've done your own small part like me to soil,
not sometimes felt a purpose?

Some might shoot you for it, granted. It remains
a purpose, though, and though
I almost see you lift the gun, you may have sensed
a near-exalting rightness
in doggedly keeping at it, just as Dubber's cur
keeps at his climb, shows up.

Sydney Lea

I WAS THINKING OF BEAUTY

for Gregory Wolfe

I've surrendered myself to Mingus's *Tijuana Moods*
on my obsolete record machine, sitting quiet as I sat last night.
I was thinking of beauty then, how it's faced grief since the day
that somebody named it. Plato; Aquinas; the grim rock tablets
that were handed down to Moses by Yahweh, with His famous
    stricture
on the graven image. Last evening, I was there when some noted
    professor

in a campus town to southward addressed what he called, precisely,
The Issue of Beauty. Here was a person who seemed to believe
his learned jargon might help the poor because his lecture
would help to end to the *exploitations of capitalism* —
which pays his wage at the ivied college through which he leads
the impressionable young, soon to be managers, brokers, bankers.

He was hard above all on poems, though after a brief appearance
poetry seemed to vanish. It was gone before I knew it.
The professor quoted, *Beauty is Truth, Truth Beauty,* then chuckled.
He explained that such a claim led to loathsome politics.
I'm afraid he lost me. Outside, the incandescent snow
of February sifted through the quad's tall elm trees,

hypnotic. Tonight as I sit alone and listen, the trumpet
on *Tijuana Gift Shop* lurches my heart wih its syncopations.
That's the rare Clarence Shaw, who vanished one day, though Mingus
    heard
he was teaching hypnosis somewhere. But back again to last evening:
I got thinking of Keats composing and coughing, of Abby Lincoln,
of Lorrain and Petrarch, of Callas and Isaac Stern. I was lost

in memory and delight, terms without doubt nostalgic.

I summoned a dead logger friend's description of cedar waxwings
on the bright mountain ash outside his door come middle autumn.
I remembered how Earl at ninety had called those verdigris birds
well groomed little folks. Which wasn't eloquent, no,
but passion showed in the way Earl waved his workworn hands

as he thought of beauty, which, according to our guest,
was opiate. Perhaps. And yet I went on for no reason
to consider Maori tattoos: elaborate and splendid,
Trinidadians shaping Big Oil's rusty abandoned barrels
to play on with makeshift mallets, toxic junk turning tuneful.
The poor you have always with you, said an even more famous speaker,

supreme narcotic dealer no doubt in our speaker's eyes—
eyes that must never once have paused to behold a bird,
ears that deafened themselves to the song of that bird or any.
Beauty's a drug, he insisted, from which we must wean the poor,
indeed must wean ourselves. But I was thinking of beauty
as something that will return—here's Curtis Porter's sweet horn—

outlasting our disputations. I was thinking it never had gone.

Sydney Lea

YELLOW HOUSE

You had to know the combination.
That's how you put it: how to tweak
air volume controls on the antique pump,
and from which roof valley you needed to chop
the ice dams first, and how to get
a stone-dead boiler to kick in again.

Where to aim your propane torch
at that same damned pipe just under the sink
in the kitchen that froze to death whenever
it was twenty below, not to speak of lower.
You couldn't get things too hot too fast.
If you did, the whole cold mess would burst

at the usual elbow, and you'd have to sweat
another new joint, and the water that jetted
before you could turn the valve would have turned
to instant crackling ice on the floor.
That old fake-brick linoleum floor,
no cellar below it. You were in for it now,

but good for it too because you were young
and welcomed a challenge —no children yet
to worry about, as you did about
the Round Oak stove, all filigree
and fluted finial but its firebox only
thin sheet metal that would glow so red

you sat up to watch it, afraid for the house,
for your wife upstairs. One time there lay
just moisture enough in the sand you shoveled
to damp the blaze that the stove blew the mica
right out of its door, coals scorching the boards.
Still you survived, if the marriage didn't.

Isn't it good to be out of that wreck,
that old yellow house with its corncob and paper
for insulation, its biting boreal
gales through every socket and nailhole?
And you married again. After 25 years,
it looks as though this thing has stuck.

After this quarter century,
you're in it for good now. How strange, therefore,
that you can almost think well of those days
when most of a winter meant such an adventure.
It's better now, and your walk this morning
in the deep-blue glory of February,

planet-bright snow on every branch,
and your coming home to affection and warmth —
you couldn't beat either with a stick or stone,
as your long-dead grandmother used to say
back in a time when the drifts got deeper,
the air got colder, your children were only

dreams of a future, who are grown and gone.

Sydney Lea

My Wife's Back

All naked but for a strap, it traps my gaze
As we paddle: the dear familiar nubs
Of spine-bone punctuating that sun-warmed swath,

The slender muscles that trouble the same sweet surface.
We've watched and smiled as green herons flushed
And hopped ahead at every bend, and we've looked up

At a redtail tracing open script on a sky
So clear and deep we might believe
It's autumn, no matter it's August still. Another fall

Will be on us before we know it. Of course we adore
That commotion of color, but it seems to come
Again as soon as it's gone away. They all do now.

We're neither young anymore, to put matters plainly.
My love for you over thirty years
Extends in all directions, but now to your back as we drift

And paddle down the tranquil Connecticut River.
We've seen a mink scratch fleas on a mudflat.
We've seen an osprey start to dive but seeing us,

Think better of it. Two phoebes wagged on an ash limb.
Your torso is long. I can't see your legs
But they're longer, I know. Phoebe, osprey, heron, hawk:

Marvels under Black Mountain, but I am fixed
On your back, indifferent to other wonders:
Bright minnows that flared in the shallows,

the gleam off that poor mink's coat,
even the fleas in its fur, the various birds
—the lust of creatures just to survive.

But I watch your back. Never have I wished more not to die.

Gary Lenhart

Now and Then

"…but not in Nottingham."
Silly sad jingle sticks in mind
as a friend tells me

about his infant daughter.
I wish her childhood
as magical to him

as my daughter's
remains to me.
"The things you do for love,"

the compromises you make
with Disney's corporate product
so your child won't be alone

as inevitably she will be
dancing to a tune
of her own invention.

"My wife wants me to spend Sundays
playing Daddy, but I
don't have time for that shit.

I like to kick back and watch the Jets,"
Said one buddy. Now his daughter
grown and gone, only Jets are left

forever young. The girl grows up
and the boy stays lost
in Neverneverland.

When Wendy tries to explain
he doesn't understand.
"Oh, Peter, but I'm a woman now."

Gary Lenhart

To a Skylark

O English bird
I've never seen but
Read about so much
In English poems

Where you've had starring parts
As Nature's watch
Warning Romeo to flee
Juliet's balcony at dawn

Or as prosaic groundling fowl
I'm sure thou wert or
Hogg would never have invented
You to write about so flatly

During years when unbridled Industry
Began to destroy your habitat
On a large scale
And you were taking off

In flights of Wordsworth, Shelley,
Christina Rossetti and other glamorous
Celebrants of your heavenly ascents
Including the humble John Clare

Who saw you high in the air
But also huddling on meadow floor
Alongside your domestic partner
To escape the pranks of bully

Schoolboys en route to merchant firms—
By that time you were so high
In the poetic firmament
That Hopkins, Hardy, even Meredith

Viewed you as symbol more than bird,
Bardic inheritance invisible in flight
Instead of feathered fowl
Elusive to the flush, scarcely

More noble than the cowering rabbit.
By the time of Ted Hughes
You weren't much more than sentiment,
"As if the globe were uneasy"

An object of environmental research
On the red list, threatened species
Of homely grace
In a remnant landscape

Disappearing rapidly as the poems
Of a disappearing countryside.
Hail to you as you blithely rise
Above the fluctuating meadows!

Daniel Lusk

THE OAT BITCH & THE OLD MAN'S DAUGHTERS

It's an old story
and I suffered it.
How the patriarch fell
and the tractor fell silent.

How wind stirred
among the crowd of oat sheaves
left standing in the field

as if his spirit
waited among them.

How a stranger came
in the guise of a preacher
to lift, unwitting, the last
sheaf to the wagon.

Who bent his head to the load
in prayer or resignation.

How the sheaf-goat
dressed as a child
lifted a pitchfork to stick it
into the wagonload
as the tractor lept ahead.

How the stranger,
as in a ritual of harvest,
came to be killed.

I was that stranger. I
bled to the tines'
victorious singing. Bled
for the Oat Bitch's hunger.

They laid me down
by the howling thresher,
torn half-naked
and shorn of disguise.

Cleansed and poulticed
my body with unguents
so I no longer knew myself
or how long I died

but awoke one day to silence
and the curious balm
conferred on my wounds
by the old man's daughters.

Daniel Lusk

To the Boy Saved from Drowning

So in the days
the moss had no stones
wild turkeys picked among
ruins of winter
deer browsed the brown margins

there was only the smoke
of my fire and the Milky Way.

From nothing,
from empty slumber
great blue the preacher
knee deep in water,
tall in his tattered coat.

As it happened, I sunned
my young body on the wing dam
where the river swallowed a boy
whole and helpless as I was
at my own baptism.

I thrust my arm
into the rush of waters
and hauled him up,
dripping like a newborn
onto the thigh of the dam.

Three wives and at least
as many children, counting you.
Three bags of truth, I said.

And he rubbed his eyes,
glared at me as if I had
either pushed or fathered him.
You are the mud god himself,
he said. Now you know the truth.

Be silent, I replied. No talking.

The larger and small are singing.
The things will take it from here.

And we both
crawled off toward that
for which we had been saved.

Gary Margolis

Runner Without a Number

I didn't qualify to wear a number.
To pin one to my chest. To lean closer
to the starting line. To run behind

the flock of Kenyans. Starting in Hopkinton,
the streets lined with fans and plastic
cups, visions of finishing downtown

in Copley Square. By the church and library
in a sea of finishers. Half-thrilled. Half
in shock, tinfoil wrapped. I have to admit

I was a Boston bandit, a runner
without a number, jumping
in where I thought I belonged.

Having trained all winter at home
in Vermont. Stopping
on the dirt roads to talk

with a stranger, to pick up a wrapper.
Some days, to step across a ditch
to follow tracks across a field,

as far they went, as far as I could go.
Before I was meant to turn back, crossing
where I'd been, lost enough to find the road

again. To see myself on Patriot's Day
twenty-six miles away, a lifetime I can't forget.
Cresting Heartbreak Hill, really three hills

in one. Running by John Kelly's ghost,
in Rita Jepto's draft. Past that curb's boy,
handing me a drink from his backpack.

Gary Margolis

CHAGALL'S GIRL

I'm assigned a seat next to the new girl
from Iraq, to teach her primary school
English. I didn't ask to volunteer to point

to things and say their words.
It's Nineteen Fifty-Four again.
Still names for things I can

point to, in and out of school.
My friends look at me as if I'm
the traitor that I am. I begin to like her

sooner. Holding her hand on the yellow
paper. I can tell she thinks three letters
make a bird, this girl from her former

land. Somehow she asks me if I know
the word for magic. Showing me
her wings beneath her blouse.

My friends don't understand. Threaten
to never speak to me again.
I'm too young not to believe in

threats and *Shorbat Rumman*,
her mother's pomegranate soup,
she brings for me in her *thermos*.

That *chalice* holding hot and cold.
Two words I didn't know I knew.
Until she rose in this poem's morning,

as if she were one of Chagall's girls,
rising over her hometown, smoky
village. As if those curling leaves

were notes. And not her father yelling
to her from the parking lot, Not
my friends, taunting their recess love.

Cleopatra Mathis

CANIS

It was a small comment, wasn't it, about who they were
—that last year on the dunes when all the town talk
was of coyotes, prairie wolf in search of an ocean,

those footprints instead of rabbits' surrounding the shack
or half-sunk in the cranberry bog
just off the path. They heard the howling somewhere

behind their backs as they walked out past midnight,
singing at the top of their lungs:
abandon me, oh careless love—although they knew

the coyotes knew exactly where they were. No surprise
to either of them when they wailed unusually close
and loud on a moonless night after an argument,

this time a mean one about the dogs. For God's sake,
the dogs, how much trouble they were to him,
their feeding and whining and constant

need to go out, no matter how wet or cold. And so on
till silence set itself between them, holding stiff
as each turned away to bed. But the coyotes just outside

started up their merciless lament, as if
the entire genus called them, had bound the tribe together
in protest for their brothers. Hours they heard the keening,

both of them sleepless, that rising, falling
complaint in their ears—until he couldn't bear it, he said
I'm sorry, I can't do this anymore, and she in a rush

of understanding the exact suffering fit of it, jumped up
and closed the offending one window's
half-inch crack, and just like that

in the dead center of a moan, the coyotes
stopped their noise; what I mean to say is
the wind stopped making that heartbroken sound.

Cleopatra Mathis

SALT

All those years I went the way of grief,
      turning my stony eye on disorder, something to be cleaned
          and fixed. I was lost, scrubbing away at the hidden,

hating the vase where the fruitflies nested,
      the artful bowl that held ruined fruit.
          Throw away the rot, I said, making myself saint

of the immaculate, not knowing a thing about the soul.
      Meanwhile, little spirit, essence, psyche, anima,
          the forever-alive-but-unpinnable one

turned its gaze away, claimed a crack,
      found a rusty needle, curled up in the eye of it.
          In the pine floors alone, a million crevices,

a million particles of grit, pinch, and crumb.
      What sea in my bucket could wash the world clean?
          And who knew the soul

was right at home in dust, passing
      through every incarnation: the tiny breathing
          mite it entered in the gray swirl under the stove,

expelling itself into a draft that carried it
      into the filmy grease so lightly pocked
          on the cabinet glass. Releasing, floating down,

the soul finding the one grain of salt
      lying there under my nose. Me at the sink,
          scouring the porcelain, not seeing.

Tim Mayo

SHELTER

Whenas in silks my Julia goes . . .

When with her step, slide-step, my Amelia finally went,
no one, bedside, even thought about her clothes:

those pilled, goodwill hand-me-downs she used
to wear, which didn't flow—nor even scintillate.

I thought about the soul's betraying shelter:
her lame side limping, goose-fleshed & numb,

as her silent chugging intent lugged her spirit,
its brave vibration, over cobble and curb,

body propped by a cane & the crutching weight
of a silver colored brace which bent her leg back

hyperextending the slow lope of her gait
into an unwilling liquefaction of limb.

Others saw some shaded piece of air
rise like a smoke ring: perfectly formed.

Tim Mayo

SELF-STORAGE

It's not really the self that's in there—
more like all the forgotten parts of your life
you intended to revisit:

the swimming trophy you crawled miles to win
or the gold stars on a third grade calendar
marking the few days
of the one week in your life you behaved.

Then there's those pants
you think you'll sweat yourself back into.

They lie folded among the paste trinkets of time,
the jewels of your memory.

But what if you could ...
just cinch up the whole girth of your life,
then flatten your beliefs
right out of your gut

(ironing out those wrinkles you keep stumbling over)

and fold your whole kit and caboodle of a body
(brain included with all its loose connections)

into some old snakeskin suitcase lying around
with its rusty lock and faulty hinges, then wait

the long humble moment it takes
to, at last, be carried away?

Kerrin McCadden

PASSERINES

I want to tell you about the thud against the back door,
        that my man says, "bird." That later we see its tail
        sticking out from underneath the siding. That its
        tail feathers shine like oil, shifting purple to blue,
and we are kneeling on the wet decking. The yellow
        of its stomach making it something more
        than the brown birds everywhere, a tiny prize
        for kneeling there, for prying back the vinyl siding
to find a yellow-bellied flycatcher, its cheek bloodied.
        I want to tell you how he held it, said "Passerine"
        before it took flight. Little Passerine. Songbird.
        Before she left, I brought my daughter to Saint-Jeannet.
There were swallows like boomerangs near dark,
        like here, like everywhere I go. I want to tell you
        about the neighbor, the scientist, who said they were
        swifts, not swallows. Swallows are Passerines,
but swifts are not. *Passerine,* I thought, *Passerine—*
        a more future verb tense for *to pass,* a tense I can't
        know yet—a passing I can't understand. The order
        Passerine is a mess, the scientist said. It's impossible
to track its evolution. I want to tell you I don't understand
        evolution, any of it, even mine, becoming the mother
        I will be next, the one who lets go. Once, I stood
        on a bridge and a man taught me to call sparrows to eat
from my hands, told me he was a sinner, that what he did for me
        was atonement, which is a thing I might understand.
        I want to tell you there is nothing like their tiny grip,
        the way they quiver while they peck at your palm,
wanting to fly out of reach. I want to tell you what happened
        when I let her go, but I don't understand it yet. I want
        to talk about this morning, the little yellow bird in sudden,
        dizzy flight. The trees full of yellow. How I lost sight.

Kerrin McCadden

THE DEAD

They worry I won't keep the graves when they're gone.
See my mother brushing off her hands

at her mother's grave, surveying lots,
approving and disapproving care and neglect,

my father deep in thought. The trees above
them are the gods of Massachusetts, big-

handed and quiet, tall fathers approving
the play of children in the yard. Somehow

the graves meant new stories about who was buried
underneath, our dead becoming more real,

not only more gone. When I walk with the dead here,
in my village, I want them to say more than their names

and relations, lambs on children's stones, more than
the dates that must mean influenza, or some

illness that doesn't kill us anymore.
I don't want to walk the rows anymore wondering

what shape stone I want, which says more,
the obelisk or the square, marble or granite,

and am I the wife of someone, or am I not.
I want something to happen here, some kind

of story. Maybe the little ghost from my house
will pick up her dress and run to show me her name,

or a flood will wash away the riverbank
—and a knot of bones. Or, slow motion, a hand

will work its way up through the grass—something
the graves can do to us, the way they trip

me when I walk over them, the soil a bit
lower where they have settled, these long dead

I can play whimsy with, unlike the dead
my parents will be, unbearable and new.

Ellen McCulloch-Lovell

THE BETWEENNESS OF THINGS

Just before the new year was due
things started to shake free,
stars from sky, trees from roots, rocks from ground,
streams from sides until the landscape
looked both familiar and strange.

Even air and light
moving in particles and waves
began to change, quivering
in the periphery of sight.

Light slipped into darkened rooms
and lit like butterflies on beds,
silent winds hurled circles of snow at windows,
riverwater thickened over sunken rocks,
roadside cliffs heightened overnight, their waters
fell and froze green on granite walls.
Night hardly receded, only scattered
for a few hours then settled in again.

Air tasted like water,
wind looked like stars,
stars flew out of constellations
and blew west.

Trees slipped long ridge lines
then when eyes fixed them,
stopped and stood still.
Just beyond the body's limits
nothing stayed the same

but fled fugitive from ken
except for persistent waiting

which senses the betweenness of things
until they snap back into shapes and names
in their grasp of necessary belief.

Ellen McCulloch-Lovell

LEAVING

Leaving the Capitol in a yellow cab,
no sleek sedan this time with driver uniformed,
a helicopter's low tone turns me
to see two Whitetops.
I'll remember them always, in tandem,
the din, the whirl, ripped leaves
and landing. I hugged my speech file to my blouse
held my hair down, and watched him disembark
with smart salute, the groomed grass
bending down, dog dashing out.

"What airline?" the cabbie asks.
I find a twenty, haul my black bag
out of the trunk, and soon am looking
out my oval window, glancing back.

I once stood behind the door
of the Red Room, and when
the announcer known as The Voice of God spoke,
I switched on my lavalier,
and stepped onto the red carpet.

The day before Inauguration's
dawning damp,
boxes packed for the Archives,
empty risers on Pennsylvania Avenue,
tanned Texans in full-length furs
walk the blocked-off street, I
flash my blue pass, my six-sided pin. It is
the last day I can enter. "We will always
let you in," the Secret Service guard lies, laughing.

Hovering, huge, flown above
the languid flags of the obelisk,
low toward the big white house,
helicoptors zero in.
Men crouch black on the flat roof.

There goes the president.

Ann McGarrell

The Snow Cat

Now new snow blurs the tracks
I've barely read:
Squirrel and deer; the alko's lady's
polydactyl cat, each print a seven-petaled flower.
By the first poplars they're all going. Gone.

Kneedeep in anything is shit.
Turn back. It's time.
The scraps of fur and bone
I saw last spring
are scattered deep by now,
are not

at all.

I plunge back up the hill,
no good at country, winter, death;
knowing the bears are right:
curl silently to sleep,
wear a white wreath of breath.

In my throat
the dead cat
spreads her claws.

Ann McGarrell

From a Neutral Country

For days and days kept on writing you
from a neutral country, an urgent letter
precise and present as a Swatch,
spelling it out, wanting to make sure
you understood.
           I tore it up.

Too many words to tell you
what I hope you know–
I loved you irreparably.
Regrets? Beaucoup. Toujours.

Now, perpend:
75 years ago, in another canton,
Rilke sighs adieux
to Balthus' raging mother.
Her soft breath: his starch.
Noli me tangere. Her tears.
Peonies flung down, bruised against rainy tiles.
Things broken. Keepsakes gone.
Our citrus-scented nights.
A knowing child.

And so it somehow is
that a girl with a cat swoons back in dusty light
forever, watched by a fierce dwarf.

Should you in autumn enter
rooms like these, where yearning chokes the air,
remember me: I am the manatee,
out of her depth and yours,
offering a kiss.

William Meredith

PARENTS

What it must be like to be an angel
or a squirrel, we can imagine sooner.

The last time we go to bed good,
they are there, lying about darkness.

They dandle us once too often,
these friends who become our enemies.

Suddenly one day, their juniors
are as old as we yearn to be.

They get wrinkles where it is better
smooth, odd coughs, and smells.

It is grotesque how they go on
loving us, we go on loving them

The effrontery, barely imaginable,
of having caused us. And of how.

Their lives: surely
we can do better than that.

This goes on for a long time. Everything
they do is wrong, and the worst thing,

they all do it, is to die,
taking with them the last explanation,

how we came out of the wet sea
or wherever they got us from,

taking the last link
of that chain with them.

Father, mother, we cry, wrinkling,
to our uncomprehending children and grandchildren.

William Meredith

A COUPLE OF TREES

The two oaks lean apart for light.
They aren't as strong as lone oaks
but in a wind they give each other lee.

Daily since I cleared them I can see
them, tempting to chain saw and ax—
two hardwoods, leaning like that for light.

A hurricane tore through the state one night,
picking up roof and hen-house, boat and dock.
Those two stood: leafless, twigless, giving lee.

Last summer ugly slugs unleafed the trees.
Environmental kids wrote Gypsy Moths Suck.
The V of naked oaks leaned to the light

for a few weeks, then put out slight
second leaves, scar tissue pale as bracts,
bandaged comrades, lending each other lee.

How perilous in one another's V
our lives are, yoked in this yoke:
two men, leaning apart for light,
but in a wind who give each other lee.

Nora Mitchell

CURSIVE

The girl writes *girl* and *girl* and *girl*,
a row of girls, each *girl* alike,
then leans down, surprised by the words

on the page. She touches a shape
the way she'd stroke a pet's smooth fur,
and the spindly blue creation

starts to stumble away from her
across a blue-veined, snowy plain.
One leg drags behind with knowing

what got left in the small houses
on the far side of the mountain.
She draws volcanoes in the margin,

a quivering grammar of stone.
Each girl, so young, stashes something
on the back side of flashing teeth.

Why'd you make me a girl, they ask.
Each one looks back at the mountains
turning their beautiful blue shoulders.

Form is destiny, distance form.
Girl dragging across a valley,
girl fleeing over mountains,

girl jammed in the craw of the world,
girl cawing, her gorge rising,
girl, girl, girl, girl.

Nora Mitchell

ACCELERATION

You go back into the music
and pick up the novel

you put aside when I arrived,
its two bright flaps pressed

printside down into the sofa.
In lamplight (through the window) your face

hovers over the page,
someone in the book says,

I think we're going
the right way now, so you

no longer hear the cellos
or the horns,

you're in another
state and county, snow

tumbles thickly
through the headlights,

slanting toward me
faster and faster.

Peter Money

WOWING THE GODS OF EPHEMERA

In your palm,
    the tiny balloon of a hand
        that once was liquid in a womb,

the involuntary halting of breath
    at the sight of Northern Lights
        or a tide's archival landscape,

the momentarily stunned raccoon on your front steps—or deer,
    paused in contact, of human eyes inside deer eyes,
        & deer inside human,

that stream beside Eva's house—quietly part of a cycle
    —where cows chewed & filled their udders,
        before winter's water released

the statues, feeding our livingness
    & our desire;
        where earth hangs over itself,

overcome with its own weight of being, or teasing,
    & defies the odds & wows the gods of ephemera.
        & just

as the universe contains surprises,
    flesh stupefies flesh
        & flesh does not complain.

Peter Money

ALL THE LITTLE LOSSES

The losses pile up "like 'change'"
and you use it

against your will, "like 'Time'"
as the snow falls down

on the daffodils, covering spring itself
like a sheet you did not want to see

or feel, the scrim blades stick through,
sheaths of grass like second life,

as soul—there again, a word left
on high—while we avoid the shroud

if it's only a page that will be unwritten.
Swirl "in the 'figurative'" changes

to squall and we who are human wail
as if the weather is about something else.

It is. It is about papers, the past due,
the *hurry-hurry*, the hurdy-gurdy

of our lungs. Beyond skid and accident,
beyond "natural 'death'," age, cancer,

language formed by lips and tongues,
sound resonating, moaning, from the cave

of the forming seed. We who survived,
or we who gave away, whisper and hand

in goodbye. Well, along comes time again
& you are there—tan branches inked with

the ash of the fallen—and goodbye
just turned to hello, as you stand looking at snow,

again snow, something light as sheets.

William Mundell

Butchering the Pig

We gave him first the Judas grain
To supper, while the one took aim
To make the idiot of his brain.
All haste, while drooling dim, his life
Wasting in rush of pulse, the knife
Struck, gulping to his pulsing vein.
He seemed to taste his bitter cup,
Meekly and chasten-eyed looked up
To hands that cared for him again.
Insensibly the harsh hook hung
A barb beside the tender tongue
To drag him to the hanging-tree.
Our burden felt a stone so great
We marveled who could move such weight
After we laid him rosin-clean.

William Mundell

Hill Journey

The field-bound castle, in the mirrors of their eyes,
Bear me up to the haunted hills and would
Follow me over the wall and the topmost rail
To hear the hillside wind go over the shed of pines
And walk in the acorn-fall on the runs of the deer.
I am lost about orchard and field, and leaves like apples
Are shaken by the wand of my hand down to a carpet of light.
I make songs out of the notes of ripe berries;
I sit at the hallowed tables of unharvested stumps
And drink from the earthen cup of the blue-sky spring.
I walk round roads of fallen trees through valleys of fern
And rest on islands of ledges above the waves of moss.
I read the revelations of the day
On the parchments of silver birches
And time sits with me in the hammocks of stone.
I shall go down again to the valley of concern;
I shall return to the rage of change
But it is today to the rage of change
But it is today that is forever and forever,
And I can hold the sun and the moment still
In the wink of my eyes.

Dennis Nurske

DOMODOSSOLA

We woke early, my father and I,
to hike into back country.
He had no need of a path.
Star-shaped alder leaves,
minnow-slim elm leaves,
hairy and gray in the half light,
parted to let him pass.
I followed. Surely I fitted
into that long methodical stride
like the minute hand in the hour?
Still in worked land,
we passed a dray horse
snaffling and pissing in sleep.
Geese complained bitterly
when we encroached on their pond.
Then the forest with its four storeys:
oak, cedar, mountain ash, moraine.
We climbed the spine of a dry waterfall.
When we came to the snow line
he took my hand. I had to skip,
shivering and comforted.
The lakes of that cirque
are so cold, you see your face
create itself: drop a pebble,
watch yourself shatter
and calmly re-assemble.
At noon we came to the summit
in time to hear a bell echo.
With pity we looked down
at the smoke-wisps, thread-roads,
minute oxen ploughing stamp-fields.
Did it happen just once, or always,
that he settled beside me and folded

his stiff legs, to peel
a blue veined hard-boiled egg?

When we finished a heel of bread
he strode by a path he alone knew
into the mountains of the air,
and I scrambled down, breathless,
with the shell in my pocket.

Dennis Nurske

FLORA OF THE BOREAL FLOOR

The child insisted on being carried
to touch the pine, the oak, oak, pine,
and I grew numb under that adamant voice.
My arm throbbed as she tried to decide:
Cone? Acorn? Needle? Leaf?
It's only thanks to the half light
that we can go home, she prancing
on my shoulder, trying to braid
my wisp of hair, singing absently.
Thrush or vireo, loud and invisible,
slurring two maniac notes:
wherever it calls from is the center.
Lake behind the scrim of alder
like a plenitude you long for
all your life, most of all at the end.
Lit window like a force
you can't imagine knowing you
but it consumes you without reflection.
World like a hole to fall into
forever, or else a curtain
you might stick your hand through.
Soon even she will tire of her song,
how it meets itself coming and going,
the vast spaces between notes,
the snarky refrain, Damariscotta,
the first faint stars, and she'll put
her sticky hand over my eyes: pine.

April Ossmann

What Is Metaphor For?

For an hour, metaphor
is a shovel I dig fertile soil with,
      discarding rocks and clinging roots
            I sever and remove, like lies

I'm weary of, but can't dispose of—
shifting them to fill
      another hollow or indentation
      my imagination's deemed unsightly,

disturbing a brown toad,
      who hops realistically away,
          as I alter the shape
of another gardening station

      whose reality I plan
to level. I keep digging, thinking
I'll find truth and have
          no further use for stories,

but truth is the hole I've dug, the hole
I've determined the depth of,
      the hole I'm free
to grow an imagined reality in.

April Ossmann

Juno's First Fly-By

I'm ready to visit Jupiter's
  blue north pole

I imagine awash
  in Soul—so used to storms,

he can't help but sing
  while he strums,

of wind and stinging sleet
  as god-sent destiny—

whose clouds have shadows
  some watery source

must shimmer under—
  whose rainbowed

southern aurora
  Juno recorded along

with his Alt-Blues,
  more ghostly or godly

than whale songs—
  response to the call

we fear to make.
  NASA wants to know

if this gas giant's
  core is solid,

but I don't see either
    as static reality—

change, however slow
    remains a universal constant.

If I hold my hitching thumb
    aloft to beckon Juno,

will she fly by for me,
    eager as she must be

for close-ups of her husband,
    even though his radiating fire

wards off touch—like you—
    like a virgin groom she must woo

for a millennium or two
    before they consummate.

Robert Pack

OLD MAN WALKING

We could conceive that all the conditions for the first production
of a living organism [existed] in some warm little pond ... that a
compound was chemically formed ready to undergo more complex
changes.

—CHARLES DARWIN, *letter to Joseph Hooker,* 1871

It's balmy April and the maple buds,
All swollen red and now prepared to burst
Beckon me forth to make my first spring hike
Across the field and down the woodland path
To sit beside the overflowing stream
And watch its eddies and its swirls, its crests
When leaping over stones, its spume and spray,
Its rainbow mist that arcs the scene.
            I'll sit on a smooth outcropping of rock,
Entranced by light reflected from wet stones,
Light shimmering where water undulates,
Staring at the stark spectacle without
Insignias or token of my friends
Who've died within the year; I will return
To see curled water swoop within itself,
To dwell upon the wafted splash of light,
Determined only to observe. Maybe
Old legs can't carry me so far this year;
Maybe I'll pack my lunch, but then turn back
Before I reach the stream if my hip won't
Obey my will's command; maybe for me
A final age of dwindling has begun,
And I'll return home with my blood subdued,
With disappointment shadowing my eyes
And only memory to serve as light,
My friends receding as I think of them,
Compelled to mull about origins,
How water is our universal womb.

My fear was accurate, although I tried
I couldn't make it to the chosen stream
And had to rest upon a rotting log before
I headed back, vowing to try again
In May or June, inspired, as Darwin was,
By "grandeur," nature's blind ability
To fabricate new complex forms, grandeur
Contending with profound dismay at nature's
Wastefulness—famine and violence,
An unrelenting process that began,
So awe-struck Darwin would surmise, merely
By random chance in some warm little pond
According to a shift in chemistry.
            Well, I'm not ready to give in to gloom;
Perhaps next month with the incentive that
The fullness of spring blooming brings,
Bounty exceeding ravenous decay,
I'll give my legs and hip another try
To hike me to the stream. I've gotten fond
By now of all my groping body parts,
Although no longer can I count on them
As once I could, just to enjoy, to be
Aware I am aware, to be in touch—
With what exactly I don't know, to watch
The spume play on the surging water that
Still seems to welcome the indifferent light.

Robert Pack

RONDO OF THE FAMILIAR

Beside the waterfall,
by the lichen face of rock,
you pause in pine shade to remember blue
for drawing back, and green
for trust, replenishing yourself
among familiar leaves
with scattered sunlight.
And beyond those trees in time not ours,
you see our children search
for what we gave them, only to find
our love again in other hands and faces
where our bodies cannot go.
And I step forth
into the scattered light
where you elude me,
though my hands reach out
to share these daily losses,
each beloved breath rounded to a pause,
that still compose our lives.
And the waterfall spills on;
and lichen holds to the rock-face
in the slowness of its quiet life, deliberate
as the dividing of a cell;
and you remember blue
for each round pause you made
freshening a bed,
washing a window with even strokes.
And I step forth
into quickening light
that restores you and
takes you away, telling my hands
to be true to their green truth—
as our children, preparing
faithfully to depart

beyond those trees,
hold for an instant in the pause
you have composed for them.
And I enter that pause,
though the waterfall spills on,
and pollen dust stains
our windows, and the familiar bed
deepens its repeated sigh,
as you wait for me,
each loss fragrant in your arms,
blue as the early crocus
our children soon will stoop to,
pausing by a waterfall
in familiar time beyond us
in pine shade
by the lichen face of rock.

Grace Paley (Vermont Poet Laureate, 2003-2007)

Autumn

1

What is sometimes called a
  tongue of flame
or an arm extended burning
  is only the long
red and orange branch of
  a green maple
in early September   reaching
  into the greenest field
out of the green woods   at the
  edge of which the birch trees
appear a little tattered   tired
  of sustaining delicacy
all through the hot summer   re-
  minding everyone (in
our family) of a Russian
  song   a story
by Chekhov   or my father

2

What is sometimes called a
  tongue of flame
or an arm extended   burning
  is only the long
red and orange branch of
  a green maple
in early September   reaching
  into the greenest field
out of the green woods   at the
  edge of which the birch trees
appear a little tattered   tired

of sustaining delicacy
all through the hot summer   re-
   minding everyone (in
our family) of a Russian
   song   a story by
Chekhov or my father on
   his own lawn   standing
beside his own wood in
   the United States of
America   saying (in Russian)
   this birch is a lovely
tree   but among the others
   somehow superficial

Grace Paley

House: Some Instructions

If you have a house
you must think about it all the time

as you reside in the house so
it must be a home in your mind

you must ask yourself (wherever you are)
have I closed the front door

and the back door is often forgotten
not against thieves necessarily

but the wind   oh   if it blows
either door open   then the heat

the heat you've carefully nurtured
with layers of dry hardwood

and a couple of opposing green
brought in to slow the fire

as well as the little pilot light
in the convenient gas backup

all of that care will be mocked because
you have not kept the house on your mind

but these may actually be among
the smallest concerns   for instance

the house could be settling   you may
notice the thin slanting line of light

above the doors   you have to think about that
luckily you have been paying attention

the house's dryness can be humidified
with vaporizers in each room and pots

of water on the woodstove   should you leave
for the movies after dinner   ask yourself

have I turned down the thermometer
and moved all wood paper away from the stove

the fiery result of excited distraction
could be too horrible to describe

now we should talk especially to Northerners
of the freezing of the pipe   this can often

be prevented by pumping water continuously
through the baseboard heating system

allowing the faucet to drip drip continuously
day and night   you must think about the drains

separately   in fact you should have established
their essential contribution to the ordinary

kitchen and toilet life of the house
digging these drains deep into warm earth

if it hasn't snowed by mid-December you
must cover them with hay   sometimes rugs

and blankets have been used   do not be
troubled by their monetary value

as this is a regionally appreciated emergency
you may tell your friends to consider

your house as their own   that is
if they do not wear outdoor shoes

when thumping across the gleam of their poly-
urethaned floors they must bring socks or slippers

to your house as well   you must think
of your house when you're in it and

when you're visiting the superior cabinets
and closets of others   when you approach

your house in the late afternoon
in any weather   green or white   you will catch

sight first of its new aluminum snow-resistant
roof and the reflections in the cracked windows

its need in the last twenty-five years for paint
which has created a lovely design

in russet pink and brown   the colors of un-
intentioned neglect   you must admire the way it does *not*

(because of someone's excellent decision
sixty years ago) stand on the high ridge deforming

the green profile of the hill but rests in the modesty
of late middle age under the brow of the hill with

its back to the dark hemlock forest looking steadily
out for miles toward the cloud refiguring meadows and

mountains of the next state   coming up the road
by foot or auto the house can be addressed personally

House!   in the excitement of work and travel to
other people's houses with their interesting improvements

we thought of you often and spoke of your coziness
in winter   your courage in wind and fire   your small

airy rooms in humid summer   how you nestle in spring
into the leaves and flowers of the hawthorn and the sage green

leaves of the Russian olive tree   House!   you were not forgotten

Grace Paley

On Mother's Day

I went out walking
in the old neighborhood

Look! more trees on the block
forget-me-nots all around them
ivy   lantana shining
and geraniums in the window

Twenty years ago
it was believed that the roots of trees
would insert themselves into gas lines
then fall   poisoned   on houses and children

or tap the city's water pipes   starved
for nitrogen   obstruct the sewers

In those days in the afternoon I floated
by ferry to Hoboken or Staten Island
then pushed the babies in their carriages
along the river wall   observing Manhattan
See Manhattan I cried   New York!
even at sunset it doesn't shine
but stands in fire   charcoal to the waist

But this Sunday afternoon on Mother's Day
I walked west   and came to Hudson Street   tricolored flags
were flying over old oak furniture for sale
brass bedsteads   copper pots and vases
by the pound from India

Suddenly before my eyes   twenty-two transvestites
in joyous parade stuffed pillows under
their lovely gowns

and entered a restaurant
under a sign which said   All Pregnant Mothers Free

I watched them place napkins over their bellies
and accept coffee and zabaglione

I am especially open to sadness and hilarity
since my father died as a child
one week ago in this his ninetieth year

Grace Paley

That Country

This is about the women of that country
Sometimes they spoke in slogans
They said
>   We patch the roads as we patch our sweetheart's trousers
>   The heart will stop but not the transport
They said
>   We have ensured production even near bomb craters
>   Children let your voices sing higher than the explosions
>   of the bombs
They said
>   We have important tasks to teach the children
>   that the people are the collective masters
>   to bear hardship
>   to instill love in the family
>   to guide the good health of the children (they must
>   wear clothing according to climate)
They said
>   Once men beat their wives
>   now they may not
>   Once a poor family sold its daughter to a rich old man
>   now the young may love one another
They said
>   Once we planted our rice any old way
>   now we plant the young shoots in straight rows
>   so the imperialist pilot can see how steady our
>   hands are

In the evening we walked along the shores of the Lake
                of the Restored Sword

I said   is it true? we are sisters?
They said   Yes, we are of one family

Jay Parini

THE INSOMNIAC THINKS OF GOD

       Midwinter, after midnight:
coyotes shrill the bitter valley
as the owl, in moon-tones,
wonders who. Far off,
the lonely engine of a plane drones on.

It's then I think of him
who, unlike me, is without boundaries,
who, unlike me, can hold his tongue.
He listens urgently,
whose wakeful ear outlasts the night.

Jay Parini

Dead Reckoning

In a red November's sunset mood
I move among the dead in this late wood,
old friends or family: a world gone by —
their dates, encapsulated, lifted high.
They shine around me, infinitely full
of what they were. One of them, a fool,
grins stupidly from distant ear to ear.
I'm silly as a boy when he comes near
with his loose tongue, those sassy lips,
a bag of tricks and well-worn quips.
One ghostly girl breaks down in silt,
her smell of mud, sharp taste of salt:
all shade and shadow, dangling vines
and roots that dig into the moldy, pine-
tar soil. It's painful to recall her fleshly ways,
the lilting manner of her easy sway,
her snow-bright bloom, or how she balanced
in the high-wire winds I rarely chanced.
I walk among the long familiar shades—
progenitors, accomplices, and aids.
Like there, my father, in a sandy mound,
his love like water running underground.
He takes a quiet place among these dead,
these whisperers in my unquiet head,
who sift in currents, humming in the wind,
and almost without bidding come to mind,
small lights that shimmer, lead me down
this dusky path so thickly overgrown
I have to wonder if I'll make it back
before the sun turns cindery and black.

Angela Patten

Ever Since Breaking My Wrist

I've noticed that the woodpecker
hopping from deck rail to deck rail
to reach the suet-cage looks somehow—
armless—and the raven picking
seeds up from the snow, bright eyes
darting this way and that, appears—
vulnerable—on two spindly legs
like a prisoner in handcuffs
or a card-sharp nailed for dealing
from the middle of the deck.

It is always disarming to see a bird in flight.
The great blue heron perched on one leg
like a battered armature takes off
crying out his *cawchee* in disgust.
We look up from our fiberglass canoe
to see him suddenly become sprung
rhythm, great wings beating the wind
in a slow disdainful dance.

John James Audubon loved birds so much
he sometimes killed a dozen
before finding the perfect model
then pinned it down with wires to create
a lifelike image of a bird in flight.

And though my Kevlar-covered broken wing
will heal in time, I still rejoice that birds
can take their leave of us without regret
by pulling the ace of flying from their sleeves.

Angela Patten

"The Singel Bridge at the Paleisstraat in Amsterdam, 1896"

title of a painting by George Hendrik Breitner

At that time in busy Amsterdam
the day divided neatly into threes
like strands of braided hair.

In the mornings maidservants dressed in drab
ran errands back and forth across the bridge,
all the small dogs of Holland
yapping at their heels.

On winter afternoons between eleven and four,
wealthy ladies went shopping,
tripping lightly in their button boots
over the slippery surface of the bridge.

Evenings prostitutes appeared,
dark shapes along the balustrade
like black tulips wilting
on the *Aalsmeer* auction floor.

In this most waterlogged of cities
three deftly separated streams
proceeding toward the sea.

The painter's penchant was for street life
and the purposeful endeavors of the poor.
Like the maid he captured for an artist's study
as she hurried home across the bridge,
her figure framed against the back-lit buildings,
the sky gravid with impending snow.
But in the Rijksmuseum she no longer
looks like all my ill-used aunts and grandmothers

who spent their lives in service to the rich.

Instead she dominates the canvas,
a massive figurehead in lavish fur-trimmed cloak
and high black hat with spotted veil—
a sleight of hand to please a wealthy patron.

And perhaps to give her—for posterity
at least—eternal afternoon.

Verandah Porche

KITCHEN HINTS: NOT TO ENTER
WINTER EMPTY-HANDED

1.

Hold a candle to a mirror.
Spell out the lover's name in tallow.
Dip a spatula in water.
If brittle letter-blobs chilled on silver
won't lift evenly set him aside.

2.

Fill a black sky-speckled kettle
with a rolling boil. Steam quart jars.
Can light. Seal and cool.

3.

Take a cleaver to red cabbage.
Thunk! Choose half. Ink its imprint:
dense violet strata
curved around a geologic core.
Pull yourself together.
Shred the clean side
for a tart slaw. Serve.

4.

Root for your future.
Bring daughters into wind.
Bend to the field.
Watch their white hands
numb and gladden
around red potatoes.

Dig for our ancestors.
See with your fingers.
Quick work.
Frost's no false alarm.

5.
Squash song
Simmer forever my delicata:
two-toned thick-skinned winter keeper.
Why take a lifetime to be tender?
Beside you the wet seeds burn.

Verandah Porche

W (I DO) W

1.

C lose S have
D awn's n early w hit e ::
The m our ning dove's
Lame n tat ion
A wed by dear th
The w id ow s crawls
Th rough her o ration
Unt ether ed t ouch ::
His g host t hum bs
On her stern um
Pres sing :: Love is
T here d anger of
Dr owning? So me

2.

No D read R egret

In dependence Eve ::
F ire works cr own his
G rave all heave n breaks

Loose foil ed strata gems
S tar s pang led
Ri sing & glow e ring ::

O c rest fallen l over o pen
My lack l us ter hear t
To the *om* in boo m!

Carol Potter

Bear Hunting in North America

> *99 percent of my poems flew into the ether*
> *because I didn't write them down fast enough . . .*
> —*Ruth Stone*

There you were chatting on the radio as if you
hadn't been dead for a week. I was driving
and weeping what I hadn't wept for a long time

even for my own mother. How startling it is to
hear the dead speak after they're gone.
When I got to work, I sat in the parking lot

watching the sky clear and the lake get
smooth as glass. And what of those poems
out there in the ether, Ruth? If I were to stand

at the lake's edge, tilt in just the right direction,
might the metal in my mouth pick them up?
Might the skin? Might the hair on my head?

Might this heart? You hear about people
getting radio stations in their teeth. Signals
they just can't explain. Yesterday, in the field

below my house, three bear hunters out calling
and whistling for their dogs. The men were holding
metal contraptions into the sky—looked like bicycle

baskets with aluminum foil patches hanging every
which way. The men were tracking their dogs.
The dogs were out there somewhere in the woods,

whooping. You could hear them rising up over
one ridge, disappearing down the next. They had
their own business. Places they needed to get to.

Carol Potter

What Moves

What moves might eat you or save you. Might be
    what you were looking for all along or what was looking for you
the whole day. What moves. The leaves on the trees. The dog
    across the field, then rolling in something dead. To keep it. Mark
it. Let anyone coming along behind him know it was his. Then later
    finding a skull and chewing on it. The dog as grave-digger.
As place-keeper. Sound asleep when the coyotes put up their yell
    from that crack in the earth coyotes call from. What moves
will be something alive. Is alive. Is the water tumbling
    through the trees and you need the water. Your own mother
diving into it wherever she could find it. You learned to drink.
    You drank from her though she sat quite still while you did it.
What moves is what you need. The sky spackled at the top
    of the hill. The wind that came blowing down. The sky.
That wind poking at the house. What moves might eat you
        or save you.
The water you dove into to grab your mother who had dived into
    something much too shallow to be diving into. The water your
mother's mother dove into to pull the child from the water
    though it was too late. How still that child was in your
        grandmother's
arms. How still your mother was when she was watching it.
    Your grandmother laying the child down in the sand. How the
        water
kept on moving like nothing had happened. How the sky kept on
    moving. How the breath moved in and out of all the people's lungs
come to see the child lying still on the sand. How still your mother
    was when she left you. When she pulled that last breath out of the
        room.
How what moves might save you or eat you. How
    quiet. How like the sea would be if it stopped. How stopped.
How quiet. What saves us. What eats us.

Elizabeth Powell

From The Book Of Condolences

The book forewarned: *You may have visions.*
You may think you hear your dead parents speaking in the courtyard.
On page fifteen it comforted: *Life is a process of second guessing*
   oneself.
It uncannily predicted: *You may be completely screwed.*
It offered irony and canned laughter: *Ha, ha, ha.*
It gave dubious advice: *Wait. There may be a way out, but the door has*
   premonitions and is very fragile.
It asked: *Knock, knock. Who's there?*
On the cover, a picture: *The dead tiptoeing, startled like ballerinas.*
The book warned: *It is the pain of the absence of the body you will fear.*
It provided a clue: *Beware of a goblet filled to the brim with agony.*
It whistled: *The far water remembers. It pools and sings of the*
   ransacker.
The punch line was always: *Do not drink the story.*

Elizabeth Powell

At The Swatch Watch Store In Newark's Terminal C

I'm going home.
I look at Swatch watches
at a store of timepieces for people who wait.

Once there was a purple inside space called deep of night
where God's amygdala made time. The Newark moon
did not shine. No travel delays, all fine.

The past kept living inside me
like a cheap Timex.
"Where are you going?"

the store clerk said. But I heard my father in my head,
practically dragging me from bed to bon voyage me
out of Newark when this terminal was merely stairs,

no moving sidewalks, when we were people still,
not consumers, flying nineteen dollar flights into Burlington,
Vermont on People's Express.

"Get your ass on the damn plane."
My long dead father still waving me goodbye, his Barry White
voice in a bubble
floating above me like a cartoon, or a synapse or brain protein.

"You're making me late for an important meeting."
Scotch still in my pores like milliseconds
collecting for takeoff into minutes. O, briefcase:

The Wild Blue Yonder song he used to sing me.
On my own. Then. Now. A store of timepieces
for those who wait. Once Amelia Earhart dedicated

this airfield and hangar. Deep inside God's amygdala,
I tick-tock. "I'm going. I'm going"
　　　And he's gone into a parade of pinstripes into the vast importance

of commerce. I hold a swatch watch. It has a big cherubic face
　　　that says 11:11. The angels are watching.
They haven't aged. My hand to God's portal.

Alison Prine

Naming the Waves

Above the harbor these clouds refuse to be described
except in the language with which they describe themselves.
I stand here in the morning stillness.

Which is of course not a stillness,
the sky spreading open in the east with amber light
while drifting away to the west.

Here I can sense how the world
spins us precisely in its undetectable turn
somehow both towards and away.

The blue of the harbor holds
the sky in its calm gaze.
This is a love poem, be patient.

Between you and me nothing leaves,
everything gathers.
I will name for you each wave rolling up on the harbor sand:

> *this is the first breath of sleep*
> *this the cloth of your mother's dress*
> *this the cadence of our long conversation*

I want to show you how everything
on this harbor has been broken:
shells, glass, rust, bones and rock —

Crushed into this expanse of glittering sand,
immune to ruin, now rocking
in the slow exhale of the tide.

Alison Prine

THE ENGINEERS TAUGHT US

to check one hundred times a day
and tomorrow we will keep on checking.

Everything is here: messages, filters, compass,
wisdom, music, news of the world,
time of day everywhere. Locators.
Something of my old life—the childhood
neighbor's laugh, burned patch
from the shag rug of 1979, phone numbers of the dead.

When I admitted that for months after his suicide
I left my brother voicemails,
my sisters all said they had called him too.
We are believers.

Dear engineers, please
put me in touch with those
who have trespassed against me.

The fortune teller will not take the engineer
to be her lawfully wedded wife.
Together they will not provide
the navigation tools to fill me
with a greenhouse of hibiscus.

My smartphone offers no shelter.
There is only building from the inside
and its necessary loneliness.
It's a terrible machine that won't
let me loose.

Julia Randall

Appalachian

Light on these leaves November makes
that was a yellow year your face
Hyannis, Truro, and the house
needlequick, seaspoiled, moors a piece.

As seasonless as sands must keep
I in this gold mosaic care
to send sight only, only sight
after the southward drift of things.

Who with her closer heart would dare
commit the falling of that fire
perform the brute historian?

The thicket history of wings
November makes, and ashes own
the sycamore's decline from green.

Julia Randall

The Coast

How, arriving from the waste,
the heart leaps to the guiding coast.
Without the eyes' assurance
even our instruments and natural talents
are poor props in the random troughs
of hills and waters. Crest on crest,
planet on planet tries the chart of space.
Even savage rocks,
after plans passed or surf run,
miles of sluggish river, years of stars,
even the rocks' rude direction
settles our task. There will be dunes to cross,
cliffs, entering bays. But north, south, east, or west,
their line sets out a continent, bounds a home
for inland exploration.
                         May I return,
thus, from the wilds of absence, where I lose
feature, being one with all the elements,
wave with the drifted wave, or light in air,
blown seed with seeds, straight to edge and center
of all my maps, my saving break in space,
my love: not Caribee to Columbus
gives better name, or locates wandering faith
more sure than the wished-for dangers of your face.

Adrienne Raphel

The Ambassador

I am the ambassador to Paris, China,
I took a gondola to Tibet.
Wonderful wedding light.
So clean I can't breathe.

I am the ambassador to the boy with a curse
from the old country. His hands press his chest.
What about Ouija boards,
     —I burned one in the park.

> *The middle of America*
> *The malls decay and fall*
> *Big Mouth Billy Bass*
> *Sings on the wall*

> *Zambonis gold with mold*
> *Fish tanks filled with stuff*
> *The Colosseum was a woods until*
> *It was the Colosseum*

I have an ambassadorship, it's a token.
I ambassador Monopoly.
I'm the banker,
and I embargo everything.

> *The edges of America*
> *The malls decay and fall*
> *Big Mouth Billy Bass*
> *Moans on the wall*

> *Zambonis plastic from Japan*
> *Fish tanks empty, cracked*
> *The Colosseum is alive tonight*
> *With many hungry men*

I am the ambassador to a crash.
They give me a bomb to hold.
They also give me a Ouija board.
It's not the one you sold.

> *Empire America*
> *Something decays, falls*
> *Big Mouth Billy Bass*
> *Shrieks on the wall*
>
> *Sibyls on Zambonis*
> *Fish tanks filled with gods*
> *The Colosseum is for rent*
> *You'd better get in line*

I'm your astrological ambassador.
I found you in another mind.
You've been there a long time,
You're here, too.

> *The porches of America*
> *Sidewalks strip and fall*
> *Big Mouth Billy Bass*
> *Thumps on the wall*
>
> *Fur-tailed dogs chase plastic balls*
> *Fish tanks stuffed with men*
> *Magnets of the Colosseum*
> *Waiting for the fridge*
>
> *The metros of America*
> *Escalators fall*
> *Big Mouth Billy Bass*
> *Is silent on the wall*
>
> *Cathedral Nova Zembla*
> *Fish tanks blank with gunk*
> *Colosseum credit card*
> *You haven't got a check*

Adrienne Raphel

NOTE FROM PARADISE

Somewhere in a Spain I think of as France
dozens of geese live in Paradise.
They run at the river,
swaying their sizeable livers,

while on either side I think there are
fields and fields, or one, of lavender,
faced blue toward the sun,
lavender first and by far.

It is late summer, early winter.
That spleenish November, another
idea altogether. It was something like flying.
Well, it was very like something,

the geese with their orange oversexed feet
bumping each other.
And enormous grasshoppers leaping,
clutching their back haunches.

In every way this is the peaceable kingdom,
the geese are livers. It's fall. It's spring.
Things migrate here. It's too far.
Also the grass, too hot by far.

A mushroom flaps around a stumpy tree,
underbelly brown where it hits the sun.
Something supposed to be seen
is seen. Something's supposed.

Into the grasses, into the wheat,
the worms have got into the flour,
the green, green worms in their bright, bright skin
colors, berserk in the heat,

Leap in the bergamot, latch to the barleycorn,
leap to the three-pointed clover
no crops here cropped close as your lover,
no time here till the corn.

What am I but a half-life
what do I do but I have
to do, to face these fields where they are
lavender first and by far.

F D Reeve

A Bar at the Folies-Bergere

Excessivley naturalistic
—Roger Fry

Unbridled pleasure seems undemocratic
especially if it's stamped with royal cachet.
Some say the long-lost past was aristocratic
(time, too, has its fashions of the day).

Does history contradict itself? Well then, it does.
Rose-peddled faces smile in pantomime
like lovers shaking with each other's news.
Deaf women run about like ordinary fools.

The pure-in-heart applaud from Paradise.
And the very rich behind their opera glasses
watch the night tremble over the pit, then rise
with the moon above the naked masses

writhing under the chandelier
like drunken carp in a pond.
The barmaid is lapis lazuli;
her eyes, two wet, black stones.

O dark excesses! Unnatural love!
Cold weather's necessities!
St. Anselm's silly proof!
Frock-coated dolphins mock the sea.

Ladies, take off your pearly dresses!
Here comes the serpent again.
The forbidden tree is heavy
with fruit and surrounded by hungry men.

F D Reeve

Venus, Half Dressed

Wet and nude like a fish, she lies back;
the curve of her spine sings *Alive, Alive-o!*
With the lips of your eyes you kiss her soft hip,
her thigh, her plump calf, each half-painted toe
        like a magnet drawing you into love.

Is this the woman who turned the heads
of old men in Troy? Achilleus's prize
Agamemnon stole? Velasquez's friend
who, in exchange for immortality,
        slept with the artist every night?

Look! A boy has captured her face
in his mirror. There, three figures meet.
Time flows like water over soft gray silk.
Space fills with her breasts. In the blue distance
        dawn breaks in the perfect sky.

Mark Rubin

ESTHER

Yet again the late night sex whines of two
porcupines in my apple tree. Their creed,
Often Wrong but Never in Doubt,

is counterintuitive to my own
clumsy how-do-you-dos. I temper
skin hunger with magical thinking,

the need to see three times a lovely
in three settings before courage
to say, *Excuse me, we haven't met, but . . .*

A ridiculous man knows best to practice
greeting animals he can hold in his hand,
for starters, *Bufo americanus,* the plump

bumpy toad whose hop is more
statement of fact than leap of faith.
A man at last at peace

with his own girth welcomes the waddle
of a red-orange newt, intent
on getting who knows where, its four short legs

like a self-contained relay team. Burdened
by love for small things that move
and big things that move through me,

I keep my disclaimer and creed
to myself, as any itchy man would do when
on two occasions he sees someone toss

pigeon crumbs from a crinkled bag
stored in her purse. A respite from minding
my own business, I wanted badly to mind

hers, to say, *I like pigeons too. They're like
urban chickens, but lighter on their feet.*
And might have had I not then

been reminded of Esther, my pet
Bantam, whom I saw parasailing
the air's invisible life in the talons of a hawk.

The ground rooting me like a rotund seed,
it was over in a flash, all but the warmed
still air between us.

Mark Rubin

UNWHITTLED

When the time comes for my father
to inherit the earth, he has one word
for everything: *Mama. Mama*
who feeds him mango and pureéd pear.

I watch her climb into his bed, nestle
in his arms like a seed of hope
embedding so uselessly she blossoms
into acceptance, into what is so.

Has stopped pretending to be more
than a wife — Saint Bess the Refuser
cauterizing grief with prayer — stops
wanting more than he can bear.

It is time for the volunteer weepers
to leave us their babushkas.
They've left more water in the air
than we know what to do with,

a cup we can't refuse. Thirst
has taught us to be kind, polite,
to think of others first.
No wonder I could say the Lord's Prayer

before I could my own. Even
the wrinkled toad, master of pathos
hunched by the glass door, hops off.
Don't be fooled.

When the poor enter the Land of Ha-Ha,
they are too tired to laugh, too weak
from cheap saltines and mush.
Their pajamas don't fit

and they could care less, which forces
the rest of us to care more, to make up
the difference the rest of our days.
I begin today

by washing what's left of him
so he won't be ashamed to die.
I am nothing. In broken English
I would say, *My heart is breaking.* Instead

I gather his unwhittled pine blocks
and toss them in the fire, those
would-be birds not yet carved
by his hands, now freed by mine.

Mary Ruefle

WINTERSAULT

The corpse had a motion detector
and when you approached it
it sat up and stretched out its arms
its eyes rolled back to white
And then the most peculiar thing—
It turned its head around,
All the way around, 360,
Then said something stupid.
it wasn't gross or funny
in no way frightening
rather sweetly sad especially
when that head turned round
and reminded me of my mother
and at the thought of my mother
there was a corpse in me,
it sat up and stretched out its arms
rolled those eyeballs back
turned its head all the way around
then said something stupid
like *old long since mum.*
I give a cup of kindness away
if only I'd sung *Old Lang Syne.*
Should old acquaintance
be forgot, and never brought to mind?

Mary Ruefle

JEWELWEED

Mother and daughter
spend the summer
popping jewelweed pods.
A sensitive plant, its pods
explode at the slightest touch.
A train passes on the other side
of the river. Little girls
in the water frantically wave
their teen-age dolls, while
a woman on a towel rolls over,
while hope is in a napkin
buried in the earth like salt.
Mother and daughter touch
another pod and the lifeguard's
whistle warns the boys
not to jump from the bridge.
A single cattail holds more energy
than a ton of coal.
And at night the stars ask the day
if things aren't other than they seem.

Tony Sanders

CORDLESS

O to be telephoned late at night by a stranger whose voice
projects nothing but bright concern, nothing intimate
between you except a common regard for the hour
that passes like a game of solitaire in a dark kitchen.
Who wouldn't want the attention? The gas-blue torpor
of the range abandoned for the invisible quasar of comfort
coming from someone just as iffy on the downtown side
of your universe. The transmission of knowledge or love
might pale in contrast to a bridge built largely on talk
and silence. Cordless, you might make your way to bed
with the receiver at your ear so that when there is nothing
further to be said, no more need to console one another,
you can say goodbye knowing there is good reason
for conversation that begins in mystery and ends with sleep.

Tony Sanders

FISH AND BLOOD

Schools of mythical fish twirl in our hearts
because long ago someone stocked the pond.
Maybe there's too much data in the blood.
Not that such angling is rigged. Dice rolls
always favor the house. Yet still we bleed.
We yearn, we pine, we wave our mixed-up rods
like kid conductors in botched rehearsals,
coaxing scales again. Opportunity
knocks, an unexpected tug on the line,
or the western side of the sternum. Heart
drum. Beat of a sad man doing a dance.
Beat of frenzy as fat drips from the spit
to the fire. Hot-blooded, high-pulsed,
it is the fishermen who are cast down.

Stephen Sandy

THATCH

The man with arms who would hold them out
Might not know what a tree he seemed to be
To come for shelter to. Or then one day
he might, as chance decrees; and stop to wonder

Before an oak, inveterate huddler twisting
From storm or reaching sunward on its hill
When it found itself a kind of green veranda
For stragglers, bushed marines combing their hair,

A respite from the hot valley. This
Reticence he'd feel was like the quiet
Of a field when battle has moved onward
Elsewhere, and a strange calm on the long grass

Moves in as if earth shied, wounded, wincing;
And knelt, rooted, for nightfall and the stars.
He thought the reticence like the isolation
Of white dwarves, although a lesser, hardly

Cosmic rigor. He held himself erect.
The grass moved, the crickets in the grass
Stirred then as the grass he trod arched slowly back
Erect as it had been. Night rose; the grass,

The stonecrop, dragon's breath, the yellow asters
Rose up together from advancing shadows
Where the man walked on, imagining the refuge
He would come to, holding his arms wide now

As if to hug the stars, himself the refuge
He plodded toward, finding his body charged
With shade. The dark coursed through him, streamed beyond
Like direct current. Then he thought of those

Who came to him for shelter and how death
Was his accomplice now, the senior partner;
As once all dwellings had fire only, until
At length fire and darkness got discarded,

When men stopped watching them—began to live
In the high wattage of what they were doing.
Once everyone knew thatch, like dark, like fire,
Presences underfoot or overhead;

Everyone knew them, the rarity of them later
Was only our looking the other way. Only
The reticent man, holding his arms raised wide
Will find it as it was before it went quaint

And fossil, to be killed, like dust. Now he knows it:
Strong as wire, tender almost, a life
Surprised, because it was there all the time
Shy, smiling, asking with its dead lights.

Stephen Sandy

Four Corners, Vermont

October sun, blue sky
burning the fields sienna,
even the governor upstate
raking a lawn, his kingdom
of this world. That afternoon
on Main Street, at the four
corners, the cop was trying
to push a small bat with
the butt of his pistol from
the window-box by the door
of the Putnam Hotel, an
unused window-box
where the bat, mistaken, caught
by daylight, had fluttered down
like a fallen leaf. Three
townsmen, not doing much
but holding their own, keeping
up on the news, kept watch.
The policeman laughed, tucking
his pistol back in its
holster. The teenage bellhop
so far with nothing to do
has pitched the bat out now.
It quavers to the walk
by the rail of the hotel stairs.
The bellhop and a man
wearing a jack shirt, worn
and too small for his arms,
stomp at it, grinding their heels
between the palings. The boy
runs back inside. It is
Norman Rockwell-ish, this
tableau the passers-by
are watching. Soon the boy

is back and kneeling with
a fork. The leaves have fallen
but the day is warm; even
the governor tidies his lawn.
The boy will jab at the black
remnant, the tines will ring
out, hitting the pavement
again; again. Everyone
in the land must know his place,
any beast
of the field his lair, his own.

Jim Schley

DAUGHTER

When older herself
with hair streaked white
and sagging a little, below

will she say of me
"He was well-known," "He was well-to-do"?
(not likely)

"He knew what he wanted . . ." ?
"He was sometimes at loose ends"?
Or, if I'm lucky,

"He drove slowly enough
to miss swallowtails and frogs."

"He read to me
*Little Women, Anna Karenina,
Portrait of a Lady* and *Beloved.*"

"He baked the family's bread."

Jim Schley

Unmemorized Man

> *Life leaves us habits in place of happiness...*
> *Where is the golden certainty of my youth?*
> Tchaikovsky's *Onegin*

Old man, not so old
but with beard twigged and thready as a nest
and his chest like a slack-bellied steer's.
Impressive even now, six foot five,
one who'd give you pause.
Not my own but my wife's
addle-pated uncle, name of Ron
— as he says: *Ron Quixote,*
Man of Dementia. Our tattered knight.

He loves recitals and symphonies
as he's listening, but later ...?
Take him to dinner and a show,
when you drop him off he'll know,
but by dawn or next noon
he can't recall. *What? Where? With you?*

As he wanted his own car
(his *own*—for how long?)
I showed him the way in mine,
from one town to the next, belayed
on lit lines from headlights,
and for every few seconds looking forward
I'd peer back through my mirror to see
his hands, white-knuckled on the steering wheel,
and thrusting face, eyes held fast on my tail-lamps.

He adored the opera, and as we
descended the stairs, each with an arm

over the other one's shoulders, he said
What do they see, coupla gay guys, yah?
Out on the town. Or father and son.
A vast laugh tipped his girth,
and rain swept over us, brittle curtain
drawn across trees and old gray fields.

But: *Where's my car parked?* Then, *Which car?*
and *What road will take me home?*
Which house? What life, with which wife?

And he groaned, *I've got no rearview mirror.*
This is no joke.

Home, we were only driving home,
five miles of fog-smeared blackness,
the mass of moisture not presence or substance
but something scraped from view,
the vacuum beyond almost seen.
Only twenty years between us, and twenty feet,
while the eight tires of our two battered jalopies
whipped circles of spray like dories in swells
through a sunken, saturated place

near the cattail marsh
where a friend passed in thick mist thirty years ago
and was suddenly surrounded
by a herd of horses he had to swerve between,
and one kicked out a taillight.
Not even there, I only heard the story
but I hear a hoof crack and the shattering lens,
one of countless memories: *Carried how? From where?*

Him or me, who is who, I believe
I'm sure I know who's in the lead,
I'm in front glancing back.
My eyes in this storm, tiny lenses for a mind

not unlike a sleet-smeared, night-struck windshield
in a car with no view to the rear, driven by a man
without memory of what's behind.

Imagine how he feels: Mouse-nest of riffraff
in the inner ear; sheaves of flies' wings
under eyelids, which obscures his gaze,
and belly enlarging like a balloon pumped ever more—

But that's so fanciful. In truth, his vantage is wan.
Waking to coffee and toast. Then coffee, toast, and cold cuts.
Later gin and toast, or canned soup (a burner left on for hours),
or many nights, a carton of some fried thing. With pie.

Fugue-like, these wiper blades' staggered sweep.
The radio plays an aria from the opera we saw.
Cascades of static tumble across the broadcast like sand
circling the tight ligature of an hour glass…skidding down…

From where? Toward where?

Vijay Seshadri

MEMOIR

Orwell says somewhere that no one ever writes the real story
  of their life.
The real story of a life is the story of its humiliations.
If I wrote that story now—
radioactive to the end of time—
people, I swear, your eyes would fall out, you couldn't peel
the gloves fast enough
from your hands scorched by the firestorms of that shame.
Your poor hands. Your poor eyes
to see me weeping in my room
or boring the tall blonde to death.
Once I accused the innocent.
Once I bowed and prayed to the guilty.
I still wince at what I once said to the devastated widow.
And one October afternoon, under a locust tree
whose blackened pods were falling and making
illuminating patterns on the pathway,
I was seized by joy,
and someone saw me there,
and that was the worst of all,
lacerating and unforgettable.

Vijay Seshadri

North of Manhattan

You can take the Dyre Avenue bus to where the subway terminates
just inside the Bronx
and be downtown before you realize
how quickly your body has escaped your mind,
stretching down the tracks on a beam
until the band snaps and the body slips free and is gone,
out the crashing doors, through the stiles,
and up the long chutes,
to burn both ways at once down the avenues,
ecstatic in its finitude,
with all the other bodies,
the bundles of molecules
fusing and dispersing on the sidewalks.
Ten to the hundredth power,
bundles of molecules are looking at paintings,
bundles of molecules are eating corn muffins,
crabcakes, shad roe, spring lamb, rice pudding.
Bundles of molecules are talking to each other,
sotto voce or in a commanding voice—
"I agree with you one hundred per cent, Dog";
"I looked for you today, but you'd already gone";
"I've left the Amended Restated Sublease Agreement on your desk";
"I'm going home now,
and you think about what you did."
The ear grows accustomed to wider and wider intervals.
The eye senses shapes in the periphery
toward which it dares not turn to look.
One bundle is selling another a playback machine,
a six-square-inch wax-paper reticule
of powdered white rhinoceros horn,
an off-season-discounted ticket to Machu Picchu,
a gas-powered generator

for when the lights go out,
a dime bag of Mexican brown.
It is four o'clock in the afternoon.
The sunlight is stealing inch by inch
down the newly repointed red-brick wall.
She comes into the kitchen wrapped in the quilt
and watches as he fries eggs.
"After what just happened, you want to eat?" she says in disgust.
Will she or will she not, back in the bedroom,
lift the gun from the holster
and put it in her purse? The mind, meanwhile,
is still somewhere around Tremont Avenue,
panting down the tracks, straining
from the past to the vanishing present.
It will never catch up
and touch the moment. It will always be
in this tunnel of its forever,
where aquamarine crusted bulbs feed on a darkness
that looks all around without seeing,
and fungus, earlike, starved for light, sprouts
from walls where drops of rusted water
condense and drip.

Don't say I didn't warn you about this.
Don't say my concern for your welfare
never extended to my sharing the terrible and addictive secrets
that only death can undo.
Because I'm telling you now
that you can also take the same bus north,
crossing over against the traffic spilling out of the mall
and waiting twenty minutes in the kiosk with the Drambuie ad.
There. Isn't that better?
More passengers are getting off than on.
The girl with the skates going home from practice
will soon get off, as will
the old woman whose license to drive has been taken from her.
They will enter houses with little gazebos tucked in their gardens.

And then, for just awhile, the mind will disembark from the body,
relaxed on its contoured plastic seat,
and go out to make fresh tracks in the snow
and stand and breathe under the imaginary trees—
the horsehair pine, the ambergris tree,
the tree that the bulbul loves,
the nebula tree…

Neil Shepard

Waterfall At Journey's End
(Johnson, VT)

Yet another metamorphic
swimming hole, waterfall
where language fails.

Gneiss, schist, slate.
You can hear nouns meta-
morphose to verbs, *gnarl, shiver, split,*

then strip down, tumble
in granitic kettle-holes
and camouflage themselves

in green water, green
because pines hang
above the fault-line

and shade language
from blue-blank sky where some-
body's watching, listening

to the syllables of delight.
This is the place of pre-
delight, before the light

blinked on in our fore-
brains and pained us with fore-
knowing. No, this place

delivers a hiss, a wordless
rush through gray clefts,
the high chattering scream

of being submerged in momentary
cold so cold the body knows
undeniably, indelibly,

these are the high walls
of journey's end, of anaerobic
last-gasp, body-turning

blue. And tongues become
like limbs trying to climb
the high cliffs of death

to clutch a purchase
on exposed outcrops
where words can sink

their cleats, pitons,
grappling-hooks, inventions
that turn humans pre-

human: moss-crawler, rock-clasper,
some thing attached to cold stone
that owns no language—

micaceous, gneiss-spark,
fissile schist, granite-fault—
that goes on climbing

as if it were stone dumb,
attached by its tongue
to the thing, the very thing.

Neil Shepard

Black Fly

Despise the mosquito's
precision, its slow injection

and withdrawal. A pinprick
on the skin. We're black fury. Flesh-

fevered. Our signature's
the rose bruise. The raised welt. Slapdash

to drink in the vein's blue
rivers, immerse and rise in red.

We're gyrating shimmers
jabbing the corners of your eyes.

Do we terrify? Think
Paolo and Francesca. We're love

bites on the jawline,
behind the ear, under the knee,

back of the thigh, hidden
caresses. As Orpheus sought

Eurydice, so we
journey down, down into the skin,

into veins requiring
life's sharp oxygen to turn jewel-

red again. Who are you,
bolted behind screens, itching welts

in the shade? Fall in love
with your wounds. Follow us into

the sun, and embrace, yes,
life's bloody feast, these open wings,

the sultry fury
inside whatever really lives.

Julia Shipley

TWO EGGS

This one the color
of my shoulder in winter,
and this one, my shoulder in summer.

No seam no pock no
porthole, smooth as oil.

The surface curve:
just a tip and a buttock,

silent as a horn in the trunk,
how many times can we give

what's formed inside us—
never? Always? Once?

Julia Shipley

Tokyo, Near Ueno Station

A man sweeps with vigorous strokes
petals stuck to the street.

A grey sky hovers so close,
it finally touches my face.

Instantly umbrellas float over commuters,
I walk in a current of skirt and suits, *gaijin.*

One face nears. She stops and holds out her umbrella
so insistently I accept,

then try to give it back, but she pulls up her hood
and disappears like a pebble dropped into a puddle.

I kept this umbrella
collapsed, this story in the folded

fan of my tongue until now:
I raise its spokes, its flower-patterned nylon

above a squall of self-loathing, I take cover
in that moment—her wrist still kindling my sleeve.

Jane Shore

Mom's *Grande Baroque*

"We replace the irreplaceable." Replacements.com

You sold our mother's sterling silver
to pay off your credit card, unloaded
her entire flatware set online, plus
the mahogany chest it came in.
Those cascading roses and acanthus
crowns were too formal for potlucks.
Being the older daughter,
with first dibs on Mom's diamonds
and her choker of cultured pearls,
I didn't covet her twelve-piece service
for twelve, or have time to polish
butter knives and the dozen extra
teaspoons which, waiting for dessert,
we'd balance, for effect, on our noses.
Grateful will be the family that will
replace their missing soup spoons
with spoons of ours that we'd start
cleaning a week before Passover
and Thanksgiving; place settings
like parentheses flanking Mom's
French china, which I haven't sold,
not yet. Remember, how, after
the pilgrimage to our apartment,
traipsing through five boroughs
to the Garden State, our aunts
and uncles carried on about
the Republicans? With mouths full,
they'd argue a point until it bled.
Those voices quiet, they can never
be replaced. But Mom's flatware?
Like the twelve tribes of Israel,

let the lot be divided,
let them cross the Hudson River
and pass through exotic zip codes,
let them go forth around the world
and enter the mouths of strangers.

Jane Shore

Our Fathers

During my father's married life
he never once did the wash—
that was my mother's job.
He'd fought in WW II, so wasn't
he entitled to some pampering—
socks paired, his underwear folded,
and shirts returned from the laundry
every week, six to a box?
After our mother's funeral,
my sister and I slept in our old
bedrooms, or tried to,
opposite the shelves of yellowing
mysteries we'd read as teens.
We mothered our father: showed
him cycles and rinses, and how you
spin the dial, like a combination
lock, clockwise, but only clockwise,
stopping precisely on *Delicates*
or *Permanent Press*. Obsolete
as rotary phones, those men
learned late in their lives to iron
and wash the cup they drank from,
men who never saw the inside
of an oven, but who loved
to barbecue outside—the only one
allowed to touch the fire.

Samn Stockwell

BRIDLE

First, a little bit about me.
It's April and I have a fresh mango
in the refrigerator and vertical
seams in my forehead and a weak chin.
I was a special learner
but I got ordinary.

I kick at the splinters of me—
a mistake to say I'm solitary.
(Although when my mind wanders
I wonder if I'll ever see it again,
and then, in that case, quite solitary.)

The slumber of my days is terrific
the seas so calm bees sleep on the waves.

I want someone to grab my face
and hammer it, make something new.

Samn Stockwell

First Confession

Stephen ground my face in the snow bank
and ran to his mother's house.
Martin smelled like cow shit
and held my hand in third grade.
My best friend held a velvet postcard
of the Virgin Mary glowing in the dark.

I loved her and wanted to marry her
though she committed mortal sins.

We wanted God to keep us forever
riding our bikes over the iron bridge,
waving to our distant parents.

Bianca Stone

ELEGY WITH A DARKNESS IN MY PALMS

I feel no sense of religion except this.
Each hand like a bastard on my lap.
I am thinking of the size of a darkness in my palms
that shake out verse like emerald hummingbirds.
It is Christmas Eve in Brooklyn.
I peal an orange in the nebulous vapor
and everything is quiet.
I take toast to the window
and throw the rind at the moon
that recedes into the clouds like an iridescent testicle
into the holy lap of the atmosphere.
Today I woke up baffled.
I have been wandering in gym shorts and a sweater
the empty submarine of my apartment on Christmas Eve
like Professor Pierre Aronnax
and I do not look into it further than I have to,
I look into a glass of Sangiovese
and drink it like the red sea being sucked into a black hole
like the blood of Christ because
at our core
we are vampires who cannot stand the corporeal
and O my family
every day your love is a knockdown;
I've got my book of things that have happened on the moon,
my alter and my mind set to stun.
I'm among the officious scent of living things.
But I am reading the poems of the dead.

Bianca Stone

Making Applesauce with My Dead Grandmother

I dig her up and plop her down in a wicker chair.
She's going to make apple sauce and I'm going to get drunk.
She's cutting worms out of the small green apples from the back yard
and I'm opening up a bottle. It erects like a tower
in the city of my mouth.

The way she makes apple sauce it has ragged
strips of skin and spreads thickly over toast.
It's infamous; eating it is as close to God as I'm going to get,
but I don't tell her. There's a dishtowel wrapped around her head
to keep her jaw from falling slack—

Everything hurts.
But I don't tell her that either. I have to stand at the callbox
and see what words I can squeeze in. I'm getting worried.
If I dig her up and put her down in the wicker chair
I'd better be ready for the rest of the family

to make a fuss about it. I better bring her back right.
The whole house smells of cinnamon and dust.
We don't speak. She's piling the worms, half-alive
up in a silver bowl, she's throwing them back into the ground
right where her body should be.

Ruth Stone (Vermont Poet Laureate, 2007-2011)

MEMORY

Can it be that
memory is so useless,
like a torn web
hanging in the wind?
Sometimes it billows
out, a full high gauze—
like a canopy.
But the air passes
through the rents
and it falls again and flaps
shapeless
like the ghost rag that it is—
hanging at the window
of an empty room.

Ruth Stone

TENACITY

Can it be over so soon?
Why, only a day or so ago
You let me win at chess
While you felt my dress
Around the knees.
That room we went to
Sixty miles away—
Have those bus trips ended?
The willows turning by,
Drooping like patient beasts
Under their yellow hair
On the winter fields;
Crossing the snow streams—
Was it for the last time?
Going to meet you, I thought
I saw the embalmer standing there
On the ordinary dirty street
Of that gross and ordinary city
Which opened like a paper flower
At the ballet, at the art gallery,
In those dark booths drinking beer.
One night leaning in a stone doorway
I waited for the wrong person,
And when he came I noticed the dead
Blue color of his skin under the neon light,
And the odor of rubbish behind a subway shed.
I sit for hours at the window
Preparing a letter; you are coming toward me,
We are balanced liked dancers in memory,
I feel your coat, I smell your clothes,
Your tobacco; you almost touch me.

Ruth Stone

SPECULATION

In the coolness here I care
Not for the down-pressed noises overhead,
I hear in my pearly bone the wear
Of marble under the rain; nothing is truly dead,
There is only the wearing away,
The changing of means. Nor eyes I have
To tell how in the summer the mourning dove
Rocks on the hemlock's arm, nor ears to rend
The sad regretful mind
With the call of the horned lark.
I lie so still that the earth around me
Shakes with the weight of day;
I do not mind if the vase
Holds decomposed cut flowers, or if they send
One of their kind to tidy up. Such play
I have no memories of,
Nor of the fire-bush flowers, or the bark
Of the rough pine where the crows
With their great haw and flap
Circle in kinned excitement when a wind blows.
I am kin with none of these,
Nor even wed to the yellowing silk that splits;
My sensitive bones, which dreaded,
As all the living do, the dead,
Wait for some unappointed pattern. The wits
Of countless centuries dry in my skull and overhead
I do not heed the first rain out of winter,
Nor do I care what they have planted. At my center
The bone glistens; of wondrous bones I am made;
And alone shine in a phosphorous glow,
So, in this little plot where I am laid.

Ruth Stone

Train Ride

All things come to an end;
small calves in Arkansas,
the bend of the muddy river.
Do all things come to an end?
No, they go on forever.
They go on forever, the swamp,
the vine-choked cypress, the oaks
rattling last year's leaves,
the thump of the rails, the kite,
the still white stilted heron.
All things come to an end.
The red clay bank, the spread hawk,
the bodies riding this train,
the stalled truck, pale sunlight, the talk;
the talk goes on forever,
the wide dry field of geese,
a man stopped near his porch
to watch. Release, release;
between cold death and a fever,
send what you will, I will listen.
All things come to an end.
No, they go on forever.

Sue Ellen Thompson

FERNWOOD

tDispatching the dead mandevilla leaves
with pendulum swings of my broom,
I am back on the paths of the wooded lot
next to my childhood home.

A third of an acre at most, it had trees
that cast a terrarium's jade
over the warren of rooms ringed with stones
where we squandered our summer days.

Connected by corridors paved with dirt
packed so hard it had the dull sheen
of wood, these chambers of wavering light
were the home of the house of our dreams.

My sisters and I swept them clean every day:
the minute a leaf drifted down,
we leapt upon it with rakes and brooms,
leaving only the bare, polished ground.

Day after day we swept the earth,
perfecting our shared domicile.
For whom? Our only visitors
were the cats who made it feel wild.

Our rage for order had less to do
with the home in which we'd been raised
than with our unconscious, unspoken wish
that our world continue unchanged.

What could go wrong here? Nothing, we thought.
But something disturbed that great calm:
those summers, the side woods, our parents,
the cats—every one of them gone.

Sue Ellen Thompson

It was a Small Town

which made everything
that happened there look
huge. The holiday parades
were endless, coursing
through the streets
like floodwater.
Parties overflowed
as well, channeled
by the narrow chambers
of what had once been
watermen's modest houses.

Almost everyone who lived there
had been Somebody once.
Widowed now, or simply
retired, they inflicted
their formidable talents
on a one-room library
and small stone church.

In summer, when the town
sprayed weekly for mosquitos
after midnight, those
who remembered it was Tuesday
and brought their pets indoors
talked of it the whole next day,
inviting praise for their vigilance,
while those who'd left
their windows open
quietly prepared to die.

Low-lying and surrounded
on three sides by water, it afforded
little opportunity for harsh words

to evaporate. Instead, they often pooled
into final severings. Small disagreements
took root in the flood-softened earth
and spread like trumpet vine, dividing
entire neighborhoods into plaintiffs
and defendants. Why would anyone,

you might ask, want
to live there? Because every year
there was a day in early summer
when the first magnolia grandiflora
bent down low, distributing
its fleshy bowls to the poor and hungry,
of whom there were none and all
were lost in its vast perfume.

Ellen Bryant Voigt (Vermont Poet Laureate, 1999-2002)

Bear

pressed full-length against the screen unzipping it
for a better grip to help him help himself to the seed and the suet
slung high under the eave by the man
who has charged down from the bedroom onto the porch
in his white loincloth like David against Goliath
but only one good lung shouting swearing
and behind him the woman caught
at the lip of the lit kitchen
                        where was my sister
with her gun or would she be praying since she prays routinely
for a parking spot and there it is or would she be speechless for once
that this man so moderate so genial so unlike me
had put himself one body-length away from a full-grown bear
or would she be saying you my dear are the person who married him
which of course I did I did and I stood behind him
as he stood his ground on the ground that is our porch
                                  you can see
the marks gouged by the famous claws on the wall inside new screen
now laced by a wire trellis on which nothing climbs
a vertical electric fence one of us thinks
the bear can hear it hum from the edge of the woods
watching us like a child sent to his room as we grill the salmon
we spiked with juniper berries the other one thinks
the plural pronoun is a dangerous fiction the source
of so much unexpected loneliness

Ellen Bryant Voigt

HEADWATERS

I made a large mistake I left my house I went into the world it was not
the most perilous hostile part but I couldn't tell among the people there

who needed what no tracks in the snow no boot pointed toward me or away
no snow as in my dooryard only the many currents of self-doubt I clung

to my own life raft I had room on it for only me you're not surprised
it grew smaller and smaller or maybe I grew larger and heavier

but don't you think I'm doing better in this regard I try to do better

Ellen Bryant Voigt

Effort at Speech

Nothing was as we'd thought, the sea
anemones not plants but animals,
flounder languishing on the sand
like infants waiting to be turned—
from the bottom we followed the spiral ramp
around and up, circling the tank.
Robert, barely out of the crib,
rode his father's shoulders, uttering
words or parts of words and pointing
ceaselessly toward the water, toward
one of the many shapes in the water,
what he could not name, could not describe.
Starfish, monkfish—not fish—catfish,
sea hare, sea horse: we studied the plaques
for something to prompt him with,
but he tucked his head as if shamed.
So I left them at the school of the quick
yellow-with-black-stripes conventional,
passed the armored centenary
turtle going down as I went up,
seaweed, eels, elongate gun-gray suede
bodies of the prehistoric sharks
transversing the reef, and headed to the top,
thinking to look down through the multiple layers.
When it first came at me, it seemed more
creature of the air than of the sea,
huge, delta-winged, bat-winged,
head subsumed in the spread pectorals—
unless it was all head—a kite
gliding to the wall between us, veering
up, over, exposing its light belly,
"face" made by gill-slits opening,
the tail's long whip and poison spine.
Eagle Ray: *cordata*, like the eagle;

it skated along the glass—
eagle scanning the sheer canyon wall,
bat trapped inside the cave,
no, like a mind at work, at play,
I felt I was seeing through the skull—
and then away.

for William Meredith

Ellen Bryant Voigt

My Mother

my mother my mother my mother she
could do anything so she did everything the world
was an unplowed field a dress to be hemmed a scraped knee it needed
a casserole it needed another alto in the choir her motto was apply yourself
the secret of life was spreading your gifts why hide your light
under a bushel you might

forget it there in the dark times the lonely times
the sun gone down on her resolve she slept a little first
so she'd be fresh she put on a little lipstick drawing on her smile
she pulled that hair up off her face she pulled her stockings on she stepped
into her pumps she took up her matching purse already
packed with everything they all would learn
they would be nice they would

apologize they would be grateful whenever
they had forgotten what to pack she never did
she had a spare she kissed your cheek she wiped the mark
away with her own spit she marched you out again unless you were
that awful sort of stubborn broody child who more and more
I was who once had been so sweet so mild staying put
where she put me what happened

must have been the bushel I was hiding in
the sun gone down on her resolve she slept a little first
so she'd be fresh she pulled her stockings on she'd packed
the words for my every lack she had a little lipstick on her teeth the mark
on my cheek would not rub off she gave the fluids from her mouth
to it she gave the tissues in her ample purse to it I never did
apologize I let my sister succor those in need and suffer
the little children my mother

knew we are self-canceling she gave herself
a lifetime C an average grade from then on out she kept

the lights on day and night a garden needs the light the sun
could not be counted on she slept a little day and night she didn't need
her stockings or her purse she watered she weeded she fertilized she stood
in front the tallest stalk keeping the deer the birds all
the world's idle shameless thieves away

Robert Penn Warren

EVENING HAWK

From plane of light to plane, wings dipping through
Geometries and orchids that the sunset builds,
Out of the peak's black angularity of shadow, riding
The last tumultuous avalanche of
Light above pines and the guttural gorge,
The hawk comes.
       His wing
Scythes down another day, his motion
  Is that of the honed steel-edge, we hear
The crashless fall of stalks of Time.

The head of each stalk is heavy with the gold of our error.

Look! Look! he is climbing the last light
Who knows neither Time nor error, and under
Whose eye, unforgiving, the world, unforgiven, swings
Into shadow.

      Long now,
The last thrush is still, the last bat
Now cruises in his sharp hieroglyphics. His wisdom
Is ancient, too, and immense. The star
Is steady, like Plato, over the mountain.

If there were no wind we might, we think, hear
The earth grind on its axis, or history
Drip in darkness like a leaking pipe in the cellar.

Robert Penn Warren

GRACKLES, GOODBYE

Black of grackles glints purple as, wheeling in sun-glare,
The flock splays away to pepper the blueness of distance.
Soon they are lost in the tracklessness of air.
I watch them go. I stand in my trance.
Another year gone. In trance of realization,
I remember once seeing a first fall leaf, flame-red, release
Bough-grip, and seek, through gold light of the season's sun,
Black gloss of a mountain pool, and there drift in peace.
Another year gone. And once my mother's hand
Held mine while I kicked the piled yellow leaves on the lawn
And laughed, not knowing some yellow-leaf season I'd stand
And see the hole filled. How they spread their obscene fake lawn.
Who needs the undertaker's sick lie
Flung thus in the teeth of Time, and the earth's spin and tilt?
What kind of fool would promote that kind of lie?
Even sunrise and sunset convict the half-wit of guilt.
Grackles, goodbye! The sky will be vacant and lonely
Till again I hear your horde's rusty creak high above,
Confirming the year's turn and the fact that only, only,
In the name of Death do we learn the true name of Love.

Robert Penn Warren

Timeless, Twinned

Angelic, lonely, autochthonous, one white
Cloud lolls, unmoving, on an azure which
Is called the sky, and in gold drench of light,
No leaf, however gold, may stir, nor a single blade twitch,

Though autumn-honed, of the cattail by the pond. No voice
Speaks, since here no voice knows
The language in which a tongue might now rejoice.
So silence, a transparent flood, thus overflows.

In it, I drown, and from my depth my gaze
Yearns, faithful, toward that cloud's integrity,
As though I've now forgotten all other nights and days,
Anxiety born of the future's snare, or the nag of history.

What if, to my back, thin-shirted, brown grasses yet bring
The heat of summer, or beyond the perimeter northward, wind,
Snow-bellied, lurks? I stare at the cloud, white, motionless. I cling
To our single existence, timeless, twinned.

Rosanna Warren

A Way

"The whole trick of this thing… is to get out of your own light."
—Marianne Faithfull

She said she sang very close to the mike
to change the space. And I changed the space
by striding down the Boulevard Raspail at dusk in tight jeans
until an Algerian engineer plucked the pen from my back pocket.
As if you're inside my head and you're hearing the song from in there.
He came from the desert, I came
from green suburbs. We understood
nothing of one another over glasses of metallic red wine.
I was playing Girl. He played
Man. Several plots were afoot, all
misfiring. One had to do with my skimpy black shirt
and light hair, his broad shoulders and hunger
after months on an oil rig. Another
was untranslatable. Apollinaire
burned his fingers on June's smoldering lyre
but I had lost my pen. The engineer
read only construction manuals. His room
was dim and narrow and no,
the story didn't slide that way though there are many ways
to throw oneself away.
One singer did it by living by a broken wall
until she shredded her voice but still she offered each song,
she said, like an Appalachian artifact.
Like trash along the riverbank chafing at the quay
plastic bottles a torn shirt fractured dolls
through which the current chortles an intimate tune.

Rosanna Warren

THE LINE

It's hard to see them through the lacing of forest shadows,
the old crimson blazes on tree-trunks marking the line.
Sometimes the tree has fallen. Sometimes the paint
has worn away and could be confused with lichen.
I clamber down banks, trample underbrush, pause
squinting between boughs, seeking the next mark.
The pines have scaly, lacerated bark.
Yellow birches wring crabbed hands and shudder.
I played here as a child, now I stumble
from boulder to moss hollow. Who was that girl
in raggedy summer jeans and smudged T-shirt
scrambling up granite ledges? I think I see her
slip like a coyote into older dark.
She had unevenly cropped hair, grime in her fingernails.
She crouched on a rock, mid-stream, and peered for trout,
umber quaver in the bronze-flecked flow.
And once, in shadow, kissed another girl
on the mouth, both of them wanting to know
how a boy's kiss would taste. It tasted of fear:
moist, tremulous, hovering on a brink
of territory imagined but unmarked
whose wind came muttering through branches, smelling
of balsam and leaf-mold, of creatures loosened back into the ground.

Roger Weingarten

MARBLE TOWN EPIZEUXIS

I kissed the dark
angel on her marble

cooch for luck I told
my Intro to Humanities

class forty some
years ago apropos of what

I can't remember that
got me hauled before the silver

haired English Department
Chair, whose leg was

decorated with a plaster
cast signed Geof Chaucer, and

who, after asking me to lock
the door, poured a flask of amber

liquid into a shot glass, wondering
if I wouldn't mind driving him

to the churchyard before
it turned dark. One

speeding ticket later, October's last
dead leaf slapped me

in the face as this Post-Puritan
American Lit. specialist in tweed

handed me his briefcase
and limped up to the pedestal, grabbed

her mottled cheeks for support, then,
on one burgundy wingtip, his plastered

knee like a shadow-casting sun dial
gnomon. He twirled a *Fouetté*

en tournant before he stooped for a quick
but firm professorial smooch. Losing

balance, he fell backwards—for
a moment I believed the angel

was falling too—onto my stunned twenty
plus year old self unprepared

to catch a couple
hundred pounds of academic

power that could destroy
my future in a flash. As he rolled

away, flushed
with laughter that

downshifted into sobs, he said, *When*
my wife died last winter in her sleep,

I was in a colleague's arms
at a Transcendentalism

conference in Palm Springs. I'd give
everything if

she could be here now so I
could apologize. Please

help me up, please
kill me. Please.

Roger Weingarten

Self-Portrait in the Convex Bumper of a Ford Woody

Hunched woman
in a babushka waddling

up the subway
stairs shlepping her

life in the two
bags under her eyes,

spits, *but he's*
a jew to the un

dead voice in her head. *Good*
shabbos, old

mother, I offer, and touch
a fingertip to my black

skullcap, and take a shot
at a smile. *Please, Little*

Mike, she coaxes, *carry these*
bags to the street, and if you're

nice, I'll give you a nickel. My childhood
name slashed

across her face and the pale
blue numbers of hers

tattooed to her wrist pull
the breath out of my lungs and me

back to a self
portrait in the convex

bumper of a Ford
woody easing

its way out of the gates
of a neighborhood restricted

to Jews. Toe-headed
boys toss in the back
seat, while a woman
wearing a hat and net veil

over her eyes mouths
kike through the passenger

window. My eight-year old
jaw dropped while what remained

of my childhood straddled
my bike.

Tony Whedon

Border Crossing

He'd taken some kind of awful drug the hatcheck girl
had given him and halfway through the first set the next night
things didn't add up, the other cats started looking like cats,
and so on. This wasn't the '60's and he was no longer his blazing
former self but had reverted to the regimen of the ancestors—
snifter of schnapps for breakfast, a cocktail before noon,
and now that drug she had given him. Nothing distinguished
this bar from any other but its name, Green Dolphin Street
the band had dubbed Purple Porpoise Alley, ha-ha.
"Take me home with you," she said after the gig, but
he had no home to go to. Beyond the outbuildings bulrushes
sighed and rustled in the rain, and more distant, the glow
of the meat packing plants of Cote Saint Luke and
the great Iron Fist of The North where all journeys end.

The hatcheck girl had a car, so they headed south,
his horn strapped like a corpse to the roof. At midnight
when they approached the border, lightning flickered
along the Richelieu and the customs station was brightly lit
to catch any crime. As they crossed the river bridge, a monkey—
yes, a monkey!—scrambled from the bushes in flight
from here to there, my God a monkey in these latitudes,
and when he told the border guard (who wasn't impressed)
he and the hatcheck girl were made to get out of the car.

The border guard was tall with the bulging eyes of Cerebus
who guards the gates of the Underworld to prevent those who
have crossed the river Styx from ever escaping. Thence,
the ritual humiliations sidemen suffer that haven't
made a name for themselves. As he took his horn down
from the roof of the car, he realized in horror what
that drug was the girl had given him. He washed away that
thought as he removed his trombone from its tattered case.

What a beautiful horn it was, a tarnished and dented King,
and he brought the mouthpiece to his lips. Thence
followed the years of exile in dives across Quebec,
the frozen wastes of La Belle Province.

Tony Whedon

THINGS TO PRAY TO IN VERMONT

after Robert Hass

To our Mother of Mud Season
(may she come early and be soon gone)
and the happiness of cows and the sadness
of meadows; to snow in April, cowslips and marsh
roses and bulk-tank days; to serenity,
late-winter languour, and the desire for frost;
to cicadas and Robert Frost (may he be happier and more
tolerant in his next life even if it makes him a minor poet);
to brook trout, delphiniums; and the midnight
cough of black bears sick on raspberries;
and to auxiliary verbs and to sunrise border crossings
and blizzards that last for days.
To the lonely wives of ice-fishermen
and ferryboat captains and long distance swimmers,
and to college students waiting desperately
for Spring; and to scorchers and dog days, to days that mark
the end of yearning, and others that welcome desire
and to the infinite variations of you in torn jeans
or in a summer dress, to you, the object of my desire,
and to the look of helplessness you give me
when I wake up early, early and wake you, too—
and to the grafting of seasons so we can have violets and lupine
in January, and to the preening geese, the jostling hogs
and the brilliant red crests of roosters;
to wild turkeys gobbling "Awake, awake,"
humble and undoctrinated in the ways of the domestic world—
and to the goddess who slips into my bed at a moment's notice
and then is gone with a flash of her green dorsal;
to crumbling outhouses; cool cisterns; to white mist
rising over our meadow; to barn swallows,
tanagers, snowy owls, and towhees—to the goldfinch,
the insouciant hummingbird, to luna moths

and to Islands, especially Isle la Motte
and the Shrine of Saint Anne and Malletts Bay
and to maximum security prisons throughout the state
(may they keep their prisoners secure and warm)
and to creaking bedsprings, heaving sighs, and to the lonely
postman who will bring you this letter.

Diana Whitney

SPRINGTAILS

I didn't plan to meet you in the woods—
strange mist rising from the wet snowpack,
drifting among the gray trunks, old sugarbush
drawing us back and back

to the origin of seasons, the veins of spring easing
open, running clear, black dust in our footsteps:
the first vast migration of snow fleas
working up from soil to the thawing surface,

tiny animals like scattered ash
or pepper risen to feed on sap. Wingless
they spring rashly in our tracks,
blind hope emerged to bear us witness:

one warm wet day, a window briefly open,
a window closed again and all re-frozen.

Diana Whitney

CURIOSITY

> "Resistance is useless."
> *The Hitchhiker's Guide to the Galaxy*

On the northbound lane following the river
I try to explain about horse paths, cart paths,
earth-eaters, the first dozers and rollers
laying hot tar over centuries of dirt. My daughters

still believe whatever I say, mine me
for knowledge practical and vast. *Could the moon
have a moon?* Ava asks and I don't know—
it probably could have some asteroid chip

or space-station trash snagged into orbit,
natural satellite, a crushed Coke can
or a bottle-cap. But it wouldn't last,
we can't steer the mothership, the girls want me

always in the kitchen like a planet,
steady sphere with gravitational pull,
slow burn on the horizon all night
anchoring their dreams in flannel

and cold cream; they want me cut loose
on the tramp, big crazy bounces, playing
Simon Says and Moonwalk Chase. *Curiosity*,
the Mars rover, found water in red dunes,

trace molecules, ices, thin film in fine dust.
We hunted the meteorite
deep on museum bedrock, pitted hunk of solid iron
radiant in the velvet dark, 34-ton heart

from the asteroid belt, burned into being,
four billion years old. Carmen ran
pell-mell through the Hall of Human History,
past Cro-magnon skulls and femur bones,

past DNA spiraling slow in a glass case,
to see what she'd been promised,
to lay her cheek against the cool
hard evidence of Space.

Norman Williams

Dying Dog

In the first place, we must remember that animals are entirely
spared the pain we suffer in the anticipation of death.

—Alfred Russel Wallace, *Darwinism: An Exposition of*
The Theory of Natural Selection With Some Of Its Applications

And so Old Scratch, a shepherd mix, near blind
And scabious, had no idea when
He faltered to his feet, his two front legs
Planted painstakingly, then haunches dragged
About like some medieval catapult
To launch the whole hind end, that this was it,
Lights out, *finito*; nor would it appear
He realized, stumping across the yard,
Each segment and protuberance quivering
At its own rate, like an antique tractor
Fired up but running rough, that looks as if
It might at any moment atomize,
That he would not cross back again. It seems
He simply sniffed a soporific spot
And there he took himself to drowse. We found
Him curled on withered grass now barely green,
Beside a snow bank slowly smoldering
Beneath the late March sun. Already two
Black beetles, noticing he did not flinch,
Had undertaken to investigate.

Norman Williams

VISIONING

This morning, chill. Sky lit, but sun not yet
Freed from its wooden cage of tamarack,
Jack pine, and spruce. Across the lake, mists coil
And writhe, as though a small Sargasso spawned.
We clamber on the dented scow: Borstal,
An Irish mix, and I. Painter untied,
Oars locked, I pivot, catch a crab, and lean
Lakeward, enjoying labor in small doses.

Borstal assumes his customary spot:
His rump athwart the keel, paws planted on
The foredeck like an Unwinged Victory,
With his acutest nose foremost and thrust
To scan the forest scents for fox movements
Or coordinates of bear. Catching a whiff,
He stiffens, sets, and gives the self-same growl
I've heard him give while dreaming by a fire.

I envy him his gift. I've other skills
This time of year. Let one bog maple flame,
Or wedge of geese accent the early sky,
And I can see the forest two months hence,
Soundless and gray, lit by a single glint
Of low-pitched sun between the fox-stained hill
And lowered cloud. It frightens, how it comes
All in a blink, involuntarily.

John Wood

Big Wind at Rockingham

On the hillside forgotten Puritans merge
with the earth beneath their splitting slate,
time-fractured markers cut with wigged faces
bearing wings, or children caught in alien sleep,
their young mothers remembered in a flourish
of lamentation, childbirth, and blood
all metered and rhymed in eighteenth century grief.
The big wind rises, and loose snow lifts
and whirls around their stones, crumbling now
in the passage of centuries of changeless sorrow.
What hard wind slipped and hung round them
in the gallows of their cold thought?
This high, lean church, as unadorned
as their certain pride shadows down on them
in all the cold verses of their faith.
The great, waving bushes of the yard
Shake, blossomless now, glittering in ice,
crackling in the wooing wind, whose drones
weave round the stalks like dreams
of wisping women, gowned and malign.
Or so these dead might have thought
had they stood among their stones
in this big wind over Rockingham,
where I stand among them looking out
at sweeping acres all snowed down
in the high cried winds that seem
a part of them, of their hard time
and of a set and shouldered faith.
And I think on their sculptors' dreams,
of all that winging of slate:
mere heads or heads and shoulders
or whole bodies angeling away
toward what austerity had promised,
or heaven like this cold, blown hill

in Rockingham, little better
for a reward's sake, for a blessing,
than their final compact with the soil.
In this big wind over Rockingham,
I move to the margins of their yard
and stand looking out at those sweeping acres
all snowed down, immaculate in the consolation
of winter, watching light fall warm on white hills
fall brighter than the angelic prayer,
the slate-cut hopes of sculptors, of elders,
and of their fragile, frightened children.

John Wood

My Grandson Dreams

In the night my grandson dreams
that he can fly, that he can save
his young brother and my son
from those set to harm them.
He dreams they are all together
in my son's office, there where
bad men and determined evil
have gathered for harm. And so
he lifts wild into the air, sweeping
up and down over them, breaking
their faces until bones shard and they run
howling from the sweet salves
of his angelic and ripping fury.

What cares could wrestle so innocent a rest
and drive his dreams into fear and rage?
And what can I, an old man at so many miles
from the treachery of his dreaming,
do for this little boy, who I know
would save me, as well, were I too there
in the terrible office of his dreams.

Baron Wormser

Leaving

Not to be here anymore, not to hear
The cat's fat purring, not to smell
Wood smoke, wet dog, cheap cologne, good cologne,
Not to see the sun and stars, oaks

And asters, snow and rain, every form
I take mostly for granted, makes me sad
But pleased to be writing down these words,
Pleased to have been one more who got the chance

To participate, who raised his hand although
He didn't know the answer or understand
The question. No matter. The leaving makes me sad;
So much was offered, so freely and completely.

Baron Wormser

Ode to Speech

Still fumbling with words, as if attempted eloquence
Could preserve you in my backward sight,
As if your death held other deaths at bay,
I see you emerging from the Olds Eighty-Eight,
A bandage on your head that the scarf you bought
At Liberty of London on your one trip abroad
Doesn't quite cover and you shrunken inside
Your winter coat and moving very slowly,
Tottering would be the word, though you
Were only forty-seven and trying to form a smile
Of some sort, a *desperate* smile, a smile
To rid you of pain and the weariness that
Eats my very bones, a smile to show you were
Fighting back as you taught me to fight back
When the world taunted me.
                              You halted on the sidewalk
As if to take in the cold breeze,
As if, after weeks away, weeks in a small white room,
It was a pleasure, the raw January air, how
It shoved and gnawed at a body's modest warmth.

You looked around slowly, your neck creaking,
It lately having done little more
Than propping up your cancer-besieged head,
And tried to say something, maybe about
The sky or house or our German shepherd Lady
Who wagged her tail bravely but no words
Came out, none, only a rueful blankness,
More of that stolid fumbling that was
The ruin of each laugh and kiss and exclamation.

You seemed bewildered to be there, to be alive,
To be expected to respond when all

That lay in front of you was your coming to a bed
And waiting—patient and impatient—for what the words
Nothing more to be done signified.

You'd told me you'd overheard those words—
One intern informing another.
                                        I love you all, you said
Then on the sidewalk to the dog and your husband
And us children but you didn't smile, your words
Were quiet and grave like the words in a speech
But from the depths of words, their blind insides.

Martha Zweig

Away/Home

for Marion French

Awful bad girl I was, authorities whisked me away.
Incognito: bone-meanness froze what face I had awry,
& the name they filed me by instantly forged itself an airy
dismissal, nothing to it. O sniff me, buzz me high-wiry,
nerved up: nick a socket, firefangle the razor wire
& finger the ringling & brotherly circuits, flop me, tire
me to death, but luckily I fizzled at ancient-before-my-time.
I got old. Tucked into this hairnet & nuzzled up as gentle, tame
& meek as you-know. Me, reportedly. Or one-&-the-same.
Pleased to acquaint you, I spoke up now-&-then-some:
ain't-broke a don't-fixed grin, pranced along ladylike, went home.

Martha Zweig

BOUGHBREAK

Nobody else, only the wind tipped
up & overran the easy leaf house.
Rolled up, unrolled air. The twigs twanged
ho & hum, the notch
of the world stuck at summer,
& our mother
ticked away in her green underthings
to the sky chink the breeze got in by, twinkled
a crow's eye & spun
gone & left us slung in those lofty
groin vaults to the culminating dome of living daylights.

Tirade from the cradle!—but it falls forever. I envy
bats snug in their belfry, who burst
& pour upon dusk,
all the skin-&-bones there is
aflap upon chaos, bellowing air
over the black flames at the gorge, & then every single
one of them slips back just before dawn does, & by the time dawn
tugs its web up, diffuses iridescence & flattery
into the puckering faces of water & loose
limbs of the sand,
they're all tucked in.

Contributors' Notes

PAIGE ACKERSON-KIELY is the author of two poetry collections: *In No One's Land* and *My Love is a Dead Arctic Explorer*. She is the Associate Director of the MFA in Writing Program at Sarah Lawrence College, and splits her time between New York and Vermont.

JOAN ALESHIRE grew up in Baltimore, Maryland and graduated from Harvard/Radcliffe, but has lived in Vermont, with a few interruptions, since 1963. She has published five books of poetry, and taught in the low-residency MFA Program for Writers at Warren Wilson College from 1983 to 2013. She co-founded Shrewsbury Library in her adopted hometown, and still serves the organization as a trustee. She also founded the Shrewsbury Institute for Agricultural Education, a non-profit that encourages traditional and innovative ways of farming, as well as community connections through the arts. She lives in a 200+ year old farmhouse, and has one daughter and two grand-daughters. *Days of Our Lives* will be published by Four Way Books in 2019.

JULIA ALVAREZ began her writing life with poetry, publishing *Homecoming* (1984), *The Other Side/El Otro Lado* (1995), and *The Woman I Kept to Myself* (2004). She returns to poetry often between writing novels (*How the García Girls Lost Their Accents, In the Time of the Butterflies, Saving the World*), non-fiction (*Something to Declare*) and memoir (*A Wedding in Haiti*), as well as numerous books for young readers. She is involved in several literacy & peace projects in her native land, the Dominican Republic, but is always grateful to return to her writing life in her second homeland, Vermont.

BEN BELLIT was a poet, professor, and translator who taught for many years at Bennington College. Belitt has been described by some as one of the neglected masters of the 20th century. A partial list of his books include, *This Scribe, My Hand: The Complete Poems of Ben Belitt, The Enemy of Joy: New and Selected Poems, Nowhere But Light: Poems, 1964-1969, The Double*

Witness: Poems, 1970-1976, and *Possessions: New and Selected Poems, 1938-1985*. Bellit was best know for translations of Pablo Neruda. He died in 2003.

PARTRIDGE BOSWELL's first book of poems, *Some Far Country*, received the 2013 Grolier Discovery Award. His work has recently surfaced in *The Gettysburg Review, The American Poetry Review*, and on Vermont Public Radio. Co-founder of Bookstock literary festival and the poetry/music group Los Lorcas Trio, he teaches at Burlington Writers Workshop and lives with his family in Vermont.

CORA BROOKS is the author of four books of poems, including *Rinds, Roots and Stars* (Mellen Poetry Press). She taught at Wheaton College, Goddard College and Lesley University. Her lifetime papers are archived at Harvard University. Poems of hers are permanently installed at Burlington International Airport. Cora lives in Montpelier, Vermont.

T. ALAN BROUGHTON taught for many years at the University of Vermont. In addition to four novels and a book of short stories, Broughton published nine collections of poetry, the last of which was *A World Remembered* (2010).

MEGAN BUCHANAN's poems have appeared in *The Sun* Magazine, *make/shift, A Woman's Thing* and multiple anthologies. Her first collection, *Clothesline Religion*, was published in 2016 by Green Writers Press. Born in California, Megan's lived for long stretches in Ireland, the mountains of Arizona and Vermont. Also a teaching artist and dancemaker, she often collaborates on interdisciplinary performance projects.

DAVID BUDBILL was an American poet, fiction writer, and playwright. He published eight books of poems, eight plays, a novel, a collection of short stories, a children's picture book, dozens of essays, introductions, speeches, and book reviews. His last book of poems was *Tumbling Toward the End* (2017). On March 7, 2017, Bubbill was named by the City of Montpelier as "The People's Poet of Vermont."

JULIE CADWALLADER-STAUB was born in Minneapolis, MN. She grew up with her five sisters, her parents and a dog beside one of Minnesota's lakes. Her favorite words to hear growing up were, "Now you girls go outside and play." The first collection of her poems, *Face to Face*, was published by Cascadia in 2010. Her poems have been featured on The Writer's Almanac, published in many journals, and included in several anthologies. She was awarded a Vermont Council on the Arts grant for poetry in 2001, and her poem "Milk" won Hunger Mountain's 2015 Ruth Stone Poetry Prize. She found her way home to Vermont twenty-five years ago. She lives in South Burlington and currently oversees the statewide Early Learning Challenge-Race to the Top grant.

HAYDEN CARRUTH was a poet, teacher, editor, and honorary poet laureate of Vermont. A resident of Johnson, Vermont, for many years, he wrote more than 30 books of poetry and criticism and served as the editor of *Poetry Magazine*, as well as the poetry editor for *Harpers*. He received the National Book Award for his book *Scrambled Eggs and Whiskey* and the National Books Critic Circle Award for *Collected Shorter Poems*. He was the recipient of many prizes and awards, including the Carl Sandburg Award, the Lenore Marshall Poetry Prize, the Paterson Poetry Prize, the 1990 Ruth Lilly Poetry Prize, the Vermont Governor's Medal, and the Whiting Award. He died in 2008.

DAVID CAVANAGH's four books of poems are *Straddle, The Middleman,* and *Falling Body,* all from Salmon Poetry of Ireland; and *Cycling in Plato's Cave,* from Fomite Press. David's poems have also appeared in leading journals and anthologies in the U.S., Ireland, the U.K., and his native Canada. He lives in Burlington.

DAN CHIASSON has published four books of poetry, including *Bicentennial* (2014), and a book of literary criticism, *One Kind of Everything: Poem and Person in Contemporary America.* He is the poetry critic for *The New Yorker* and teaches at Wellesley College.

CHIN WOON PING (Woon-Ping Chin) is the author of two books of poetry, *In My Mother's Dream* and *The Naturalization of Camellia Song.* Her writing has been anthologized in such collections as the *Norton anthology of Language for a New Century,* the Harper Collins anthologies of *Literature and Asian American Literature, & Writing, The City and You, Playful Phoenix, A Sense of Exile, Monologues by Women of Color, Westerly Looks to Asia,* and *On a Bed of Rice.* She received fellowships from the Pennsylvania Council on the Arts, the National Endowment for the Humanities, the Mellon Foundation, the National University of Singapore and the Pew Foundation. She lives in Vermont and teaches at Dartmouth College.

MICHAEL COLLIER's most recent collection of poems is *An Individual History* (W.W. Norton, 2012). *The Ledge* (Houghton Mifflin, 2000) was a finalist for the National Book Critics Circle Award and the Los Angeles Times Book Prize. He teaches in the Creative Writing Program at the University of Maryland and is the director of the Bread Loaf Writers' Conferences.

JEAN CONNOR served as Director of Library Development at the New York State Library, but in her retirement is enjoying a second pursuit: the writing of poetry. A graduate of Middlebury College, she lives in Shelburne, Vermont. She is the author of two books: *A Cartography of Peace* and *The Hinge of Joy* (Passager Books).

WYN COOPER's fifth book of poems, *Mars Poetica,* will appear in 2018. His poems have appeared in *Poetry, Slate, AGNI, The Southern Review,* and in 25 anthologies of contemporary poetry. His poems have been turned into songs by Sheryl Crow and David Broza, among others. He lives in Boston and Vermont, and works as a freelance editor.

STEPHEN CRAMER's first book of poems, *Shiva's Drum,* was selected for the National Poetry Series and published by University of Illinois Press. His second, *Tongue & Groove,* was also published by University of Illinois. *From the Hip,* which follows the history of hip hop in a series of 56 sonnets, and *A Little Thyme & A Pinch of Rhyme,* a cookbook in haiku and sonnets, came out from Wind Ridge Press in 2014 and 2015. *Bone Music,* his most recent collection, was selected by Kimiko Hahn for the 2015 Louise Bogan Award and published in 2016 by Trio House Press. His work has appeared in journals such as *The American Poetry Review, African American Review, The Yale Review, Harvard Review,* and *Hayden's Ferry Review.* An Assistant Poetry Editor at *Green Mountains Review,* he teaches writing and literature at the University of Vermont and lives with his wife and daughter in Burlington.

DEDE CUMMINGS studied poetry at Middlebury College (Mary Dunning Thwing Award). Her poetry has been published in *Mademoiselle, The Lake, InQuire, Vending Machine Press, Kentucky Review, Connotation Press, MomEgg Review, Figroot Press,* and *Bloodroot Literary Magazine.* She attended the Bread Loaf Writers' Conference and the Vermont Studio Center. *To Look Out From* won the 2016 Homebound Publications Poetry Prize. Her second poetry collection, *The Meeting Place,* is due out in 2019 from Salmon Poetry of Ireland. She lives in Brattleboro and is the founder of Green Writers Press.

GREG DELANTY's latest book of poems is *Book Seventeen* from LSU Press. Other recent books are *The Word Exchange, Anglo-Saxon Poems in Translation,* WW Norton; his *Collected Poems* 1986-2006, Oxford Poets-Carcanet Press. He's received many awards, most recently a Guggenheim for poetry. He is Poet in Residence at Saint Michael's College.

CHARD deNIORD is the Poet Laureate of Vermont and author of five books of poetry, including *Interstate,* (The University of Pittsburgh Press, 2015), *The Double Truth* (University of Pittsburgh Press, 2011), which the *Boston Globe* named one of the top ten books of poetry in 2011, and *Night Mowing* (University of Pittsburgh Press, 2005). He teaches English and Creative Writing at Providence College, where he is a Professor of English. His book of essays and interviews with seven senior American poets (Galway Kinnell, Donald Hall. Maxine Kumin, Jack Gilbert, Ruth Stone, Lucille Clifton, Robert Bly) titled *Sad Friends, Drowned Lovers, Stapled Songs, Conversations and Reflections on 20th Century American Poets* was published by Marick Press in 2012. He is the co-founder and former program director of the New England College MFA Program in Poetry and a trustee of the Ruth Stone Trust. He lives in Westminster West, Vermont with his wife Liz.

MARY JANE DICKERSON, UVM Associate Professor of English Emerita, has published two volumes of poems, *Tapping the Center of Things* and *Water Journeys in Art and Poetry* with artist Dianne Shullenberger. In 2015 she was a Painted Word poet at the Fleming Museum; in 2016, she and Tamra Higgins through their non-profit Sundog Poetry Center saw their "Poets and Their Craft" Series become a 2016 VTPBS featured production.

GREGORY DJANIKIAN has published six poetry collections with Carnegie Mellon University Press, the latest of which is *Dear Gravity* (2014). He was Director of Creative Writing at the University of Pennsylvania for over twenty years until his retirement in 2015 and continues to teach poetry workshops in its undergraduate program. He has summered at his house in Irasburg, Vermont since 1988.

NORMAN DUBIE, is the author of twenty-five books of poetry, most recently *The Quotations of Bone* (2015), winner of the 2016 International Griffin Poetry Prize. His other books of poetry include *The Volcano* (2010), *The*

Insomniac Liar of Topo (2007), *Ordinary Mornings of a Coliseum* (2004), and *The Mercy Seat: Collected & New Poems, 1967-2001* (2001), all from Copper Canyon Press. His newest collection, *Robert Schumann is Mad Again* will be published by Copper Canyon Press in 2019. He is the recipient of the Bess Hokin Prize from the Poetry Foundation, the PEN Center USA Literary Award for Poetry in 2002, and fellowships and grants from the Ingram Merrill Foundation, the John Simon Guggenheim Memorial Foundation, and the National Endowment for the Arts. He lives and teaches in Tempe, Arizona.

ELLEN DUDLEY is the author of *Slow Burn* (Provincetown Arts Press, Provincetown, Massachusetts, 1997) and *The Geographic Cure* (Four Way Books, NY, NY, 2007). For ten years she was editor/publisher of *The Marlboro Review* literary magazine, and lives in Marlboro, Vermont and the district of Ka`u on the Big Island of Hawai`i.

ALVIN FEINMAN (1929-2008) taught literature at Bennington College from 1969 to 1994. He was born in Brooklyn and educated at Brooklyn College, the University of Chicago and Yale. He is the author of *Preambles and Other Poems* (1964) and an expanded edition of that work, *Poems* (1990). His complete poems, *Corrupted into Song*, were published in 2016 and contain the full text of *Poems* plus 39 unpublished poems discovered among his manuscripts after his death.

KATE FETHERSTON's first book of poems, *Until Nothing More Can Break*, was published in 2012. Her poems have appeared in numerous journals, including *North American Review* and *Hunger Mountain*. Kate has been awarded Vermont Arts Council grants in both writing and visual art.

FLORENCE FOGELIN's *Once It Stops* (Deerbrook Editions, 2015), was a finalist in Foreword Press's IndieFab Book of the Year 2016 competition. Her poems have been featured on websites by *Poetry Daily* and *Women's Voices for Change*, in journals including *The Florida Review* and *Poet Lore*, and in anthologies including *Birchsong: Poetry Centered in Vermont.*

LAURA FOLEY's books include *WTF* (CW Books), *Night Ringing and Joy Street* (Headmistress Press) and *The Glass Tree* (Harbor Mountain Press). She won the 2016 Common Good Books poetry contest, judged by Garrison Keillor, and the 2016 Joe Gouveia Outermost Poetry Contest, judged by Marge Piercy.

ROBERT LEE FROST (March 26, 1874–January 29, 1963) was an American poet. His work was initially published in England before it was published in America. He is highly regarded for his realistic depictions of rural life and his command of American colloquial speech. His work frequently employed settings from rural life in New England in the early twentieth century, using them to examine complex social and philosophical themes. The winner of four Pulitzer Prizes for poetry, Robert Frost became, in the words of the critic, Safa Fatima, one of America's rare "public literary figures, almost an artistic institution." He was awarded the Congressional Gold Medal in 1960 for his poetic works and on July 22, 1961, Frost was named poet laureate of Vermont. He died in 1963, at the age of 89.

JODY GLADDING's work explores the places where language and landscape converge. She has published three books of poetry, most recently *Translations from Bark Beetle* (Milkweed Editions, 2014), and has translated thirty books from French. The poems in this anthology are part of a new collection forthcoming from Ahsahta Press.

LOUISE GLÜCK's poems are frequently described as "spare." Her first book of poetry, *Firstborn* (1968), was recognized for its technical control as well as its collection of disaffected, isolated narratives. Glück's poems in books such as *Firstborn, The House on Marshland, The Garden* (1976), *Descending Figure* (1980), *The Triumph of Achilles* (1985), *Ararat* (1990), and the Pulitzer Prize-winning *The Wild Iris* (1992) take readers on an inner journey by exploring their deepest, most intimate feelings. *Meadowlands* (1996), Glück's first new work after *The Wild Iris*, takes its impetus from Greek and Roman mythology. *Vita Nova* (1999) earned Glück the prestigious Bollingen Prize from Yale University. Glück's next book, *Averno* (2006), was a critical success and many judged it to be her finest work since *The Wild Iris*. *Poems* 1962-2012 won the *Los Angeles Times* Book Prize, and *Faithful and Virtuous Night* (2014) won the National Book Award. In 2003 Glück was named the 12th U.S. Poet Laureate. That same year, she was named the judge for the Yale Series of Younger Poets. Her book of essays *Proofs and Theories* (1994) was awarded the PEN/Martha Albrand Award for Nonfiction.She has received the Lannan Literary Award for Poetry, a Sara Teasdale Memorial Prize, the MIT Anniversary Medal, and fellowships from the Guggenheim and Rockefeller Foundations, and from the National Endowment for the Arts. In 2008, she was awarded the Wallace Stevens Award. Glück currently teaches at Yale University and lives in Cambridge, Massachusetts.

BARRY GOLDENSOHN, who lives in Cabot, is author of 8 collections of poems, the most recent of which are *The Listener Aspires to the Condition of Music, The Hundred Yard Dash Man* and *Snake in the Spine, Wolf in the Heart*, all from Fomite Press.

KARIN GOTTSHALL is the author of two full-length collections of poems: *Crocus* (Fordham University Press, 2007), and *The River Won't Hold You* (Ohio State University Press, 2014). She has also published several limited-edition chapbooks with small independent presses. Gottshall is the recipient of the Poets Out Loud Prize, the Journal/Wheeler Prize, and a fellowship from the Bread Loaf Writers' Conference. She lives in Middlebury, Vermont, where she teaches at Middlebury College and directs the New England Young Writers' Conference.

RACHEL HADAS is the author of over a dozen books of poetry, essays, and translations. Her latest book of poems is *Questions in the Vestibule* (Northwestern University Press 2016), and she is completing verse translations of Euripides' two Iphigenia plays, also for Northwestern. She is Board of Governors Professor of English at Rutgers-Newark and has spent most of her summers in Danville, Vermont for more than half a century.

WALTER RICE HARD was Vermont's most popular native poet. Born in 1882 in Manchester, Vt., he lived his entire life in Vermont, except for a few years when he attended Williams College, which he left before graduating to take over his ailing father's Manchester drug store. He began writing weekly columns for the Manchester Journal and Rutland Herald in the late 1920's, concluding each article with a free verse poem in the dialect of rural Vermont. Over the next 40 years he published nine books of poetry, along with a tourist guide he co-wrote with his wife, Margaret, titled *This Is Vermont*. Although Hard wrote mostly about Vermont, his poetry reached many outside the state's borders, appearing in such national magazines as *Life* and *Yankee*. About Hard's books, the poet Carl Sandbur commented, "They "present a likeness of a land and its people that deserves a place in the gallery of the best that has been done by the regionalists of the earth." In addition to his career as poet, Hard represented Manchester for one term in the house and four terms in the Senate. He died in 1966.

PAMELA HARRISON, winner of PEN's Discovery Poet Award for Northern New England and adjunct professor in Creative Writing at Dartmouth College, is the author of *Stereopticon, Okie Chronicles, Out of Silence*, and *What to Make of It*. A new book, *Glory Bush and Green Banana* is due in May 2017.

GEOFF HEWITT of Calais is "always playing with poems." He regularly performs in slams and readings across Vermont. Author of eight books (four of them poems), he has worked for the VT Arts Council and the VT Department of Education, and leads writing workshops and poetry slams wherever he's invited.

TAMRA J. HIGGINS, MFA, M.Ed., has taught in Vermont public schools for over 20 years and is founder of Sundog Poetry Center, Inc., a nonprofit organization that promotes poets and poetry. Her work has been published in *Prairie Schooner, Passagers, Modern Haiku, Vermont Magazine*, and other publications. Higgins is the author of *Nothing Saved Us: Poems of the Korean War* (2014) and the chapbook, *Tenderbellied* (2016). She is also co-editor of *Tasteful Traditions: A Collection of Cambridge History, Memories, and Family Recipes*. She lives in Jeffersonville.

DAVID HUDDLE teaches at the Bread Loaf School of English and in the Rainier Writing Workshop. His fiction, poetry, and essays have appeared in *The American Scholar, The New Yorker*, and *The Georgia Review*. His most recent poetry collection is *Dream Sender* (2015); and his new novel is *My Immaculate Assassin* (2016).

CYNTHIA HUNTINGTON's fifth book of poetry, *Terra Nova*, was published in February 2017. *Heavenly Bodies*, was a finalist for the 2012 National Book Award in Poetry. Currently a Guggenheim Fellow in Poetry, she holds the Frederick Sessions Beebe Chair in Writing at Dartmouth College.

MAJOR JACKSON is the recipient of a Guggenheim Fellowship, National Endowment for the Arts Literature Fellowship, and a creative arts fellowship at the Radcliffe Institute for Advanced Study at Harvard University. He has published poems and essays in many journals, and been included in several volumes of *Best American Poetry*. He is the University Distinguished Professor & Richard Dennis Green and Gold Professor at the University of Vermont. He serves as the Poetry Editor of *The Harvard Review*.

REUBEN JACKSON resides in Winooski, Vermont. He is the host of Friday Night Jazz on Vermont Public Radio, and serves as a mentor and workshop leader with the Young Writers Project. His poems have appeared in 39 anthologies, *The Montpelier Bridge,* and in a volume entitled *Fingering the Keys.* He was archivist and curator with the Smithsonian's Duke Ellington Collection from 1989 until 2009.

PHYLLIS KATZ lives in Norwich, Vermont. Her poems have appeared in *Connecticut River Review, Ekphrasis, The Salon, Bloodroot Literary Magazine, Mountain Troubadour, Birchsong: Poetry Centered in Vermont, Oberon,* and *Avocet.* Her two books of poems: *All Roads Go Where They Will,* December 2010, and *Migrations,* 2013, were published by Antrim House Books.

GALWAY KINNELL was born in Providence, Rhode Island, in 1927, and lived in Sheffield, Vermont for 43 years. He was a former MacArthur Fellow and State Poet of Vermont, and his *Selected Poems* won the Pulitzer Prize and the National Book Award in 1982. His many books of poetry include, *The Book of Nightmares, Mortal Acts, Mortal Words, The Past,* and, mostly recently, *Strong Is Your Hold.* For many years he was the Erich Maria Remarque Professor of Creative Writing at New York University. He died in 2014.

LELAND KINSEY was born and raised on a farm in Vermont's Northeast Kingdom, where his ancestors settled in the early 1800s. He conducted writing workshops for the Vermont Arts Council and the Children's Literacy Foundation at over 100 schools in New Hampshire and Vermont. Leland has worked as a farmhand, printer, and horse trainer, and taught courses at Elderhostel in writing, birding, astronomy and canoeing. He published seven collections of poetry, including *In the Rain Shadow* (University Press of New England, 2004), *Sledding on Hospital Hill* (Godine, 2003), *The Immigrant's Contract* (Godine, 2008), *Winter Ready* (Green Writers Press, 2014) and *Galvanized: New & Selected Poems* (Green Writers Press, 2016).

ADRIE KUSSEROW is Professor of Anthropology at St. Michael's College in Vermont where she teaches courses on refugees, globalization and poverty and creative writing. She is the author of two books of poetry *(Hunting Down the Monk* and *REFUGE)* published by BOA Editions, Ltd. Her current field work is in Darjeeling, India with the Stop Human Trafficking initiative in rural Himalayan villages. She is co-founder of Africa Education and Leadership Initiative along with the Lost Boys of Sudan in Vermont. She was born and raised in Underhill Center, Vermont where she lives with her family. Recent poems are forthcoming in *American Poetry Review, HIMALAYA* and *THE SUN.*

JOAN HUTTON LANDIS is the author of *That Blue Repair* (Penstroke Press, 2008). Her poems have been set to music by the composer Chris Rogerson and performed at Carnegie Hall. Poems in this book have appeared, or are forthcoming in *The Nation, The New York Times, Poetry, Salmagundi,* and in the anthology *Liberation: New Works on Freedom from Internationally Renowned Poets.* A graduate of Bennington College, Wesleyan, and Bryn Mawr, Joan lived as a young woman in France, Saudi Arabia, and Lebanon, and subsequently taught literature and poetry workshops for many years at the Curtis Institute of Music in Philadelphia, where she was Chair of the Liberal Arts Department.

ALEXIS LATHEM is the author of one full length poetry collection, *Alphabet of Bones* (Wind Ridge Books), and two poetry chapbooks. She is an environmental journalist and writing instructor at the Community College of Vermont, and her poems have appeared in *Hunger Mountain, Saranac Review, Spoon River, The Hopper,* and other journals. She lives on a small farm in the Winooski River Valley.

SYDNEY LEA was Vermont Poet Laureate from 2011-2015. Lea is author of twenty books, twelve of which are poetry; and the most recent collection of poems is *No Doubt the Nameless* (2016). He was founder and longtime editor of *New England Review.* He taught at Dartmouth, Yale, Middlebury and several European universities before his retirement.

GARY LENHART is the author of six collections of poetry, including *The World in a Minute* (2010) and *Father and Son Night* (1999) from Hanging Loose Press. His published prose includes *The Stamp of Class: Reflections on Poetry and Social Class* (University of Michigan Press, 2006) and *Another Look: Selected Prose* (Subpress, 2010).

Winner of a 2016 Pushcart Prize for his genre-bending essay, "Bomb," DANIEL LUSK is author of five published poetry collections: *The Vermeer Suite; KIN; Lake Studies: Meditations on Lake Champlain, The Inland Sea* (audiobook); *Kissing the Ground: New & Selected Poems*; a memoir, *Girls I Never Married,* and other books.

GARY MARGOLIS, Emeritus Director of Counseling Services at Middlebury College, is a Robert Frost Fellow and has taught at the University of Tennessee and Bread Loaf Writers' Conferences. His poem "The Interview" was featured on National Public Radio's "The Story." *Raking the Winter Leaves: New and Selected Poems* was recently published.

CLEOPATRA MATHIS has published seven collections of poetry. Most recent, from Sarabande Books, are *White Sea,* awarded the May Sarton Book Prize, and *Book of Dog,* which won the Sheila Motten Book Prize. Her poems have appeared widely in magazines, and journals, including the *New Yorker, The Georgia Review, The Southern Review, The Michigan Quarterly Review, Ploughshares,* and *Threepenny Review,* as well as numerous anthologies and textbooks. Awards for her work include two National Endowment for the Arts fellowships, two Pushcart Prizes, and the John Simon Guggenheim Fellowship.

TIM MAYO's second volume, *Thesaurus of Separation,* was published by Phoenicia Publishing (2016). It was a finalist for both the 2017 Montaigne Medal and for the 2017 Eric Hoffer Category Book Award. He is a six time Pushcart Prize Nominee, and the recipient of two Vermont Writers Fellowships from the Vermont Studio Center. He lives in Brattleboro, VT, where he was a founding member and organizer of the Brattleboro Literary Festival.

Kerrin McCadden is the author of *Landscape with Plywood Silhouettes*, winner of the 2015 Vermont Book Award and the 2013 New Issues Poetry Prize. She is the recipient of a National Endowment for the Arts Literature Fellowship and a graduate of The MFA Program for Writers at Warren Wilson College. She lives and teaches in Montpelier, Vermont.

Ellen McCulloch-Lovell is the former president of Marlboro College. Her book of poems, *Gone*, was published in 2010 by Janus Press and she earned her MFA in writing from Warren Wilson College in 2012. Ellen began her career as executive director of the Vermont Arts Council and then spent decades in Washington, D.C., as Senator Patrick Leahy's Chief of Staff, director of the President's Commission on the Arts and Humanities, Deputy Assistant to President Clinton and Advisor to the First Lady, and as founding director of the Veterans History Project at the Library of Congress.

Ann McGarrell, wife of painter James McGarrell, was a poet and translator who described herself as "internationally unknown." A Newbury resident, she was the author of the limited fine press book *Flora: Poems* (Perishable Press, 1990), *Revenants: A New Orleans Reliquary* with photos by Julie Dermansky (Blurb, 2008), and *Gwen and Other Poems*—a collection based on the life of the Welsh painter Gwen John (Cove House Press, 2012). Highly regarded as a translator, she won the 1997 PEN/Renato Poggioli Prize for her translation of Vittoria Ronchey's *Il Volto di Iside* (*The Face of Isis*). She died in January 2016.

William Meredith was a Consultant in Poetry to the Library of Congress, and later the Poet Laureate Consulate in Poetry to the Library of Congress. Meredith was also a Director and Chancellor of the Academy of American Poets. His many honors also included the Pulitzer Prize, the *Los Angeles Times* Book Award, the National Book Award and the Harriet Monroe Memorial Prize, the International Vaptsarov Prize, a Guggenheim Foundation fellowship in Poetry, two Rockefeller Foundation grants, and grants from the American Academy and Institute of Arts and Letters. He introduced many Bulgarian poets to the English language through his work as editor on *Poets of Bulgaria* (1986) and *Window on the Black Sea* (1992). He also translated the *Alcools* (1964) of Guillaume Apollinaire. Meredith's books of essays and criticism include *Reasons for Poetry, and the Reason for Criticism* (1982) and the highly praised *Poems are Hard to Read* (1991). Meredith died in 2007 at the age of 88 in New London, CT. The William Meredith Foundation and the William Meredith Center for the Arts continue his legacy through its residency program, poetry reading series, and various other activities.

Nora Mitchell has published two books of poetry with Alice James Books: *Your Skin Is a Country* and *Proofreading the Histories*. Her poems have been published in a number of anthologies and many journals. She has taught writing, literature, and humanities at Goddard College and Burlington College, and currently teaches at Champlain College.

PETER MONEY teaches in the Vermont State College system and is the founding director of Harbor Mountain Press. Graywolf Press published his co-translations (with Sinan Antoon) of Saadi Youssef's poems, *Nostalgia, My Enemy*. Money's other works include *Che: A Novella In Three Parts, American Drone: New and Select Poems*, and the musical collaboration *Blue Square*.

WILLIAM MUNDELL was the author of five volumes of poetry and was an accomplished artist and acclaimed photographer. The 125-member Poetry Society of Vermont unanimously elected him poet laureate in 1989, a post he shared with Galway Kinnell.

DENNIS NURKSE was born on December 13, 1949, in New Jersey, the son of Estonian economist Ragnar Nurkse. He received his BA from Harvard University in Boston, Massachusetts, and worked as a factory worker throughout the 1970s. He has also worked as a construction worker, grant writer, human rights representative to the United Nations, street musician, kindergarten teacher, translator, bartender, and harpsichord builder, among others. Nurkse is the author of ten poetry collections, including, most recently, *A Night in Brooklyn* (Alfred A. Knopf, 2012), *The Border Kingdom* (Alfred A. Knopf, 2008), and *Burnt Island* (Alfred A. Knopf, 2006).

APRIL OSSMANN is author of *Event Boundaries* (Four Way Books), and *Anxious Music* (FWB) and has published her poetry widely in journals including *Colorado Review* and *Harvard Review,* and in anthologies. Her poetry awards include a 2013 Vermont Arts Council Creation Grant and a *Prairie Schooner* Readers' Choice Award. She published *Thinking Like an Editor: How to Order Your Poetry Manuscript* in *Poets & Writers* (March/April 2011), and a biography/critical study of poet Lynda Hull in *American Writers Supplement XXI* (Charles Scribner's Sons, 2011). Former executive director of Alice James Books, she owns a poetry consulting business offering manuscript editing, publishing advice, tutorials, and workshops. She is a faculty editor for the low-residency MFA in Creative Writing Program at Sierra Nevada College. She lives in West Windsor, Vermont.

ROBERT PACK, Abernethy Professor of Literature and Creative Writing Emeritus at Middlebury and longtime director of the Bread Loaf Writers' Conference, has published eighteen volumes of poetry, most recently *To Love That Well: New and Selected Poems* 1954-2013, and five of literary criticism. In the last decade and a half, he has taught in the Honors College at the University of Montana.

GRACE PALEY was a poet, activist, and poet laureate of Vermont from 2003 to 2007. The author of several books of poetry, including *Long Walks and Intimate Talks, Leaning Forward, Begin Again: Collected Poems*, and her posthumous collection, *Fidelity*, Paley was also an activist who protested the Vietnam War, who worked with the American Friends Service Committee, and The War Resistors League. In 1969, she accompanied a peace mission to Hanoi to negotiate the release of prisoners of war. She died at home in Thetford, Vermont, in 2007.

JAY PARINI, poet, novelist, and scholar, teaches at Middlebury College. He has written biographies of Steinbeck, Frost, Faulkner, and Gore Vidal, and he recently published *New and Collected Poems: 1975-2105* (Beacon Press).

ANGELA PATTEN is author of three poetry collections, *In Praise of Usefulness* (Wind Ridge Books), *Reliquaries and Still Listening, both from* Salmon Poetry, Ireland, and a prose memoir, *High Tea at a Low Table* (Wind Ridge Books). Born and raised in Dublin, Ireland, she now lives in Burlington and teaches at the University of Vermont.

VERANDAH PORCHE, poet-in-residence, performer and writing partner, published *Sudden Eden, The Body's Symmetry,* and *Glancing Off.* "Come Over" is an album of songs written with Patty Carpenter. She received an honorary doctorate from Marlboro College. Her current project is *Shedding Light on the Working Forest,* a collaboration with painter Kathleen Kolb.

CAROL POTTER is the 2014 winner of the Field Poetry Prize for her 5th book of poems, *Some Slow Bees,* from Oberlin College Press. Potter's poems have appeared in *Green Mountains Review, Field, The Iowa Review, Poetry, The American Poetry Review, The Kenyon Review,* and many other journals and anthologies. She has recent poems in *Hotel Amerika, The Massachusetts Review, The New England Review, River Styx,* and poems forthcoming in *Field,* and in *Poet Lore.* She teaches for the Antioch University low-residency MFA program in Los Angeles, and for the Community College of Vermont.

ELIZABETH POWELL is the author of *The Republic of Self* a New Issues First Book Prize winner, selected by C.K. Williams. Her second book of poems, *Willy Loman's Reckless Daughter: Living Truthfully Under Imaginary Circumstances,* won the 2016 Anhinga Robert Dana Prize, selected by Maureen Seaton. She is editor of *Green Mountains Review,* and Associate Professor of Creative Writing at Johnson State College, and also serves on the faculties of the low-residency MFA in Creative Writing at the University of Nebraska-Omaha and Vermont College of Fine Arts Editing and Publishing.

ALISON PRINE's debut collection of poems, *Steel,* was chosen by Jeffrey Harrison for the *Cider Press Review* Book Award and was released in January 2016. Her poems have appeared in *The Virginia Quarterly Review, Shenandoah, Green Mountains Review,* and *Prairie Schooner* among others. She lives in Burlington, Vermont where she works as a psychotherapist.

JULIA RANDALL was born in Baltimore, Maryland. She studied English at Bennington College and medicine at the Johns Hopkins University School of Medicine before earning an MA from the Johns Hopkins Writing Seminars. She published seven collections of poetry in her lifetime: *The Solstice Tree* (1952), *Mimic August* (1960), *The Puritan Carpenter* (1965), *Adam's Dream* (1969), *The Farewells* (1981), *Moving in Memory* (1987), and *The Path to Fairview* (1992). An instructor at Goucher College, Towson University, and the Peabody Conservatory, among other places, Randall retired from

Hollins College in 1973 and moved to Glen Arm, Maryland. In Maryland, she was an environmental activist working for the protection of the Long Green Valley. She moved to Vermont in 1987, where she lived until her death. **ADRIENNE RAPHEL** is the author of *What Was It For* (Rescue Press, 2017), selected by Cathy Park Hong as winner of the Rescue Press Black Box Poetry Prize; and the chapbook *But What Will We Do* (Seattle Review, 2016), selected by Robyn Schiff as winner of the Seattle Review Chapbook Contest. Born in New Jersey and raised in Vermont, Raphel graduated from Princeton and the Iowa Writers' Workshop, and she currently studies literature at Harvard. **F.D. REEVE** authored more than 30 books, including 11 collections of poems, a half-dozen novels, multiple critical works, Russian translations, and plays. He abandoned an early acting career and after earning his doctorate in Russian from Columbia University, he went on to teach Slavic languages and English literature at Wesleyan University for 40 years, occasionally taking up visiting professorships at Oxford, Columbia, and Yale. Reeve was an officer of the Poetry Society of America, and a secretary of Poets House. He was the recipient of the New England Poetry Club's Golden Rose Award, an Award in Literature from the American Academy National Institute of Arts and Letters, and a D.Lit from New England College. Reeve served as Robert Frost's translator and cultural ambassador on a 1962 trip to the USSR during the Cold War. Reeve died in 2013 at the age of 84.

MARK RUBIN's poems have appeared in *The Ohio Review, Prairie Schooner, The Virginia Quarterly Review, The Yale Review*, and elsewhere. The author of one book of poems, *The Beginning of Responsibility* (Owl Creek Press), he lives in Burlington, VT where he is a psychotherapist in private practice.

MARY RUEFLE's latest book is *My Private Property* (Wave Books, 2016). She has lived in the Bennington area since 1971.

TONY SANDERS published four collections of poetry, including his latest collection of prose poems *Subject Matters* and a collaboration of verse titled *Speaking In Turn* with his friend and fellow poet Chard deNiord. Tony's poetry appeared in numerous publications including, *Poetry, Paris Review, The Yale Review, The Gettysburg Review* and *The New York Times Book Review*. Ten of his poems were nominated for Pushcart Prizes. He lived in New York City and Vermont.

STEPHEN SANDY was the author of eleven books of poetry, the most recent of which include *Overlook* (Louisiana State University Press, 2010), *Netsuke Days* (Shires Press, 2008), and *Weathers Permitting* (Louisiana State University Press, 2005). His honors include fellowships from the MacDowell Colony, the Ingram Merrill Foundation, the Lannan Foundation, the National Endowment for the Arts, and Vermont Council on the Arts. In 2006, he was awarded an Academy Award in Literature from the American Academy of Arts and Letters. He died in 2016.

JIM SCHLEY is author of the chapbook *One Another* (Chapiteau, 1999) and a full-length book of poems, *As When, In Season* (Marick, 2008). He has been co-editor of *New England Review*, editor-in-chief of Chelsea Green, and director of The Frost Place, and he's now managing editor of Tupelo Press. He lives on a cooperative in Strafford, Vermont.

VIJAY SESHADRI is the author most recently of *3 Sections*, which won the 2014 Pulitzer Prize for Poetry. He lives in Brooklyn and teaches at Sarah Lawrence College and for many years has been spending his summers in Windsor County, Vermont.

NEIL SHEPARD's sixth and seventh books of poetry were both published in 2015: *Hominid Up* (Salmon Poetry, Ireland) and *Vermont Exit Ramps II*, (Green Writers Press, Vermont). His poems appear online at *Poetry Daily, Verse Daily*, and *Poem-A-Day* (from the Academy of American Poets), as well as in several hundred literary magazines. After retirement from the BFA writing program at Johnson State College, where he and edited *Green Mountains Review* for a quarter-century, he now teaches in the MFA Program at Wilkes University and at Poets House in Manhattan.

JULIA SHIPLEY's debut collection, *The Academy of Hay* won the Melissa Lanitis Gregory Poetry Prize and was named a finalist for the 2016 Vermont Book Award. She lives in Vermont's Northeast Kingdom.

JANE SHORE's six books of poems have garnered many prizes—including the Juniper Prize (1977), the Lamont Prize (1986) and the 2010 Poets Prize. She's been a Guggenheim Fellow, a Radcliffe Institute Fellow, and a Hodder Fellow at Princeton. *That Said: New and Selected Poems*, was published by Houghton Mifflin Harcourt in 2012. A Professor at the George Washington University, she lives in Washington, DC and in Vermont.

SAMN STOCKWELL has been widely published, and her two books of poetry, *Theater of Animals* and *Recital*, won the National Poetry Series and the Editor's Prize at Elixir, respectively. Some of her poems are on the websites of *Agni, Mudlark* and *Salamander*. She has an M.F.A. from Warren Wilson College, and has taught poetry and English at the New England Young Writer's Conference, the former Vermont College and Community College of Vermont.

BIANCA STONE is a poet and visual artist, and the author of *Someone Else's Wedding Vows, Poetry Comics From the Book of Hours*, and artist/collaborator on a special illustrated edition of Anne Carson's *Antigonick*. She runs the Ruth Stone Foundation & Monk Books with her husband, the poet Ben Pease in Vermont.

RUTH STONE was born in Roanoke, Virginia, in 1915, and attended the University of Illinois at Urbana-Champaign. She lived in a rural farmhouse in Vermont for much of her life and received widespread recognition relatively late with the publication of *Ordinary Words* (1999). The book won the National Book Critics Circle Award and was soon followed by other award-winning collections, including *In the Next Galaxy* (2002), winner of the National Book Award; *In the Dark* (2004); and *What Love Comes To: New & Selected Poems* (2008), a finalist for the Pulitzer Prize. Stone's other honors and awards include two Guggenheim Fellowships, the Bess Hokin Prize, the Wallace Stevens Award, the Shelley Memorial Award, and the Walter

Cerf Award for Lifetime Achievement in the Arts. The author of 13 books of poetry, Ruth Stone died in late 2011.

ELLEN BRYANT VOIGT grew up on her family's farm in rural Virginia. She earned her BA from Converse College and MFA from the Iowa Writers' Workshop. Her most recent collections include *Headwaters* (2013), *Messenger: New and Selected Poems 1976-2006*, and *Shadow of Heaven* (2002). Her collection *Kyrie* (1995), a book-length sonnet sequence exploring the lives of people affected by the influenza epidemic of 1918–1919, was a finalist for the National Book Critics Circle award. She has also written a collection of essays, *The Flexible Lyric* (1999), and with Gregory Orr co-edited *Poets Teaching Poets: Self and the World* (1996), a selection of essays on writing. Voigt was a founder of the Goddard College low-residency MFA program, the first MFA program of its kind, and has also taught at Iowa Wesleyan College and MIT. She served as poet laureate of Vermont for four years. She has lived in Vermont for many years.

ROBERT PENN WARREN was an eminent poet and fiction writer who, for several decades, made his summer home in West Wardsboro, Vermont, where he is also buried. Warren served as the Consultant in Poetry to the Library of Congress, 1944–1945 (later termed Poet Laureate), and won two Pulitzer Prizes in poetry, in 1958, for *Promises: Poems 1954–1956* and, in 1979, for *Now and Then. Promises* won the annual National Book Award for Poetry. Warren also won the Pulitzer Prize for his novel *All The Kings Men*, making him the only American writer to win Pulitzer Prizes in poetry and fiction. In 1980, Warren received the Presidential Medal of Freedom and in 1981, he was selected as a MacArthur Fellow. In 1987, he was awarded the National Medal of Arts.

ROSANNA WARREN teaches in the Committee on Social Thought at the University of Chicago. Her most recent books of poems are *Departure* (2003) and *Ghost in a Red Hat* (2011). She was a Chancellor of the Academy of American Poets from 1999 to 2005.

ROGER WEINGARTEN writes, teaches poetry, paints, and sculpts in Montpelier. His most recent collection is *The Four Gentlemen & Their Footman.*

TONY WHEDON is the author of a poetry chapbook, three books of poetry and a prize-winning essay collection. He is a working trombone player and the leader of the ensemble PoJazz. With Neil Shepard, he founded *Green Mountains Review*. He lives with his wife Suzanne in Montgomery, Vermont.

DIANA WHITNEY writes across the genres in Brattleboro, VT. Her first book, *Wanting It*, became an indie bestseller in 2014 and won the Rubery Book Award in poetry. She's the poetry critic for the *San Francisco Chronicle* and her personal essays, book reviews and poems have appeared in *Glamour, The Washington Post, The Kenyon Review, Green Mountains Review,* and many more. A yoga teacher by trade, she's currently finishing a memoir about motherhood and sexuality.

NORMAN WILLIAMS arrived in Burlington in 1981, when duckpin bowling was still available and there was a hardware store on Church Street. He's the author of two poetry collections, *The Unlovely Child* (Knopf, 1985) and *One Unblinking Eye* (Swallow Press/Waywiser Press, 2003). During the day he works as an attorney at Gravel & Shea in Burlington.

JOHN WOOD is the author of nine books of poetry, three of which were national or international prize winners. (He twice won the Iowa Poetry Prize, and his collection *Endurance and Suffering* won the *Gold Deutscher Fotobuchpreis* in Germany in 2009). Before retiring and moving with his wife to Saxtons River, he directed the Master of Fine Arts Program in Creative Writing at McNeese from 1989 until 2006. Many of his students have gone on to win significant literary prizes as well: Stanton Fellowships, the National Book Award, the Pulitzer Prize. Wood is also a respected photo-historian and art critic. He has written many books and innumerable essays on various photographers and painters, he curated *Secrets of the Dark Chamber*, an exhibition on daguerreotypes at the Smithsonian, and he has lectured at Harvard, Vassar, and elsewhere on art and photography.

BARON WORMSER is the author/co-author of fourteen books and a poetry chapbook. Wormser has received fellowships from the National Endowment for the Arts, Bread Loaf, and the John Simon Guggenheim Memorial Foundation. From 2000 to 2006 he served as poet laureate of the state of Maine.

MARTHA ZWEIG'S work has received Hopwood and Whiting awards. Her collections include *Monkey Lightning*, Tupelo Press, 2010; *What Kind* (2003) and *Vinegar Bone* (1999), both Wesleyan University Press, and *Powers*, Vermont Arts Council, 1976. *Get Lost*, 2014 Rousseau Prize winner, is forthcoming from The National Poetry Review Press.

Acknowledgments

The editors deeply appreciate the encouragement and support of Dede Cummings, director of Green Writers Press, and Cameron Hope, editorial and design assistant. The publisher and editors gratefully acknowledge the donation of permissions from the poets in this collection.

JOAN ALESHIRE poems appear with the author's permission.

JULIA ALVAREZ poems reprinted from *Homecoming*. Copyright © 1984, 1996 by Julia Alvarez. Published by Plume, an imprint of Penguin Random House; originally published by Grove Press. By permission of Susan Bergholz Literary Services, New York, NY and Lamy, NM. All rights reserved.

PARTRIDGE BOSWELL "Husbandry" first published in *Passages North*. "Wonder" first published in *The American Poetry Review*.

CORA BROOKS "Keeping" reprinted from *Rinds, Roots and Stars: A Woman's Journal from the Great Flood* (Mellen Poetry Press, 1996). "Someone Asks You" reprinted from *Ransom for the Moon* (Acorn Press, 1978).

DAVID BUDBILL poems "Whenever" and "Reply to My Peripatetic Friends" are used with permission of the author and will appear in his posthumous collection *Tumbling Toward the End*, published in May 2017 by Copper Canyon Press.

JULIE CADWALLADER STAUB "Milk" was published in March of 2015 by *Hunger Mountain Review*. "Measurement" was published by *Spiritus* in 2013.

HAYDEN CARRUTH "Emergency Haying" and "Cows at Night" reprinted from *From Snow and Rock, From Chaos* © 1973 by Hayden Carruth, used by permission of New Direction Books. "Little Citizen, Little Survivor" reprinted from *Scrambled Eggs and Whiskey* © 1996 by Hayden Carruth, used by permission of Copper Canyon Press.

DAVID CAVANAGH "Neil Armstrong Shoots the Moon" is reprinted from *Falling Body* with permission from Salmon Poetry. "The Ice Man" is reprinted from *Straddle* with permission from Salmon Poetry.

WYN COOPER "On Eight Mile" originally appeared in *The Way Back* (White Pine Press, 2000). "Mars Poetica" originally appeared on the Academy of American Poets website as the "Poem-a-Day."

DEDE CUMMINGS "Falling Grounds" first appeard in *Connotation Press* and "Lament of the Glaciers" first appeared in *Kentucky Review*. Both are reprinted by permission of the author from *To Look Out From* (Homebound Publications, 2017).

GREGORY DJANIKIAN "Banality" first appeared in *New Ohio Review*, Fall 2015; "Mystery Farm Road" from *So I Will Till the Ground* (Carnegie Mellon, 2007).

JOHN ENGLES "Green Bay Flies," "Barking Dog" © copyright 2005 by John Engles. Reprinted by permission of University of Notre Dame Press. All rights reserved.

KATE FETHERSTON "Take Bitter for Sweet" first published in *Nimrod* and appears in *Until Nothing More Can Break* (Antrim House, 2012).

FLORENCE FOGELIN "All Men Are Mortal" appears in *Once It Stops,* 2015, by permission of Deerbrook Editions.

LAURA FOLEY "It Is Time" won the Atlanta Review Grand Prize and was first published in *Atlanta Review*. "The Orchard on Its Way" first appeared in *DMQ Review.*

ROBERT FROST "The Draft Horse," "Closed for Good," "Iris by Night," and "Wild Grapes" from the book *The Poetry of Robert Frost* edited by Edward Connery Lathem. Copyright © 1923, 1949, 1969 by Henry Holt and Company, copyright© 1936, 1948, 1951, 1962 by Robert Frost, copyright © 1964, 1976, 1977 by Lesley Frost Ballantine. Reprinted by permission of Henry Holt and Company, LLC. All rights reserved.

LOUISE GLÜCK "Bats" and "Burning Leaves" reprinted from *A Village Life: Poems* © 2010 by Louise Glück, by permission of Farrar, Straus and Giroux."The Muse of Happiness" reprinted from *The Seven Ages* © 2002 by Louise Glück, by permission of Farrar, Straus and Giroux. "The Couple in the Park" reprinted from *Faithful and Virtuous Night* © 2015 by Louise Glück, by permission on Farrar, Straus and Giroux.

KARIN GOTTSHALL "More Lies" and "Listening to the Dead" reprinted from *The river wont hold you: poems* (Ohio State U Press, 2014.)

PAMELA HARRISON "So, Caravaggio" and "Field in Snow," both first printed in *Poetry Magazine,* 1991 & 1992, respectively.

Tamra Higgins "My Father's Birth, Iowa, 1932" first appeared as "Birth, Iowa, 1932" in *Tenderbellied* by Tamra Higgins, 2016, May Day Studio.

PHYLLIS KATZ "Letter to Myself" reprinted from *Migrations* (Antrim House Press, 2013), "Curriculum Vitae at Seventy-Four" reprinted from *All Roads Go Where They Will* (Antrim House Press, 2010) by permission of the publisher.

GALWAY KINNELL "Vapor Trail Reflected in the Frog Pond" from *Three Books* © 2002 by Galway Kinnell. Reprinted with the permission of Houghton Mifflin Company. "Fergus Falling," from *Mortal Acts, Mortal Words* © 1980 by Galway Kinnell. Reprinted with the permission of Houghton Mifflin Company. "Little Sleep's-Head Sprouting Hair in the Moonlight," from *The Book Of Nightmares* © 1970 by Galway Kinnell. Reprinted with the permission of Houghton Mifflin Company. "The Bear," from *Body Rags* © 1968 by Galway Kinnell. Reprinted with the permission of Houghton Mifflin Company.

LELAND KINSEY "In the Cranberry Bog" reprinted from *Winter Ready* © 2014 by Leland Kinsey, by permission of Green Writers Press. "Fish Eggs" reprinted from the forthcoming © 2017 *Last Correspondence*, by permission of Green Writers Press.

ALEXIS LATHEM "Bergere" appeared in the Green Writers Press journal the *Hopper.*

DANIEL LUSK "The Oat Bitch and the Old Man's Daughters" first appeared in *Nimrod International Journal*. "To the Boy Saved from Drowning" first appeared in *The Louisville Review.*

CLEOPATRA MATHIS "Salt" reprinted from *White Sea* (Sarabande, 2005), "Canis" reprinted from *Book of Dog* (Sarabande, 2012).

from *In the Next Galaxy* © 2004 by Ruth Stone, used by permission of Copper Canyon Press. "Speculation" reprinted from *Simplicity* © 1995 by Ruth Stone, used by permssion of Paris Press, Inc.

ELLEN BRYANT VOIGT "Effort at Speech" reprinted from *Two-Trees* © 1992 by Ellen Bryant Voigt, by permission of W.W. Norton. "Headwaters," "Bear,"and "My Mother" reprinted from *Headwaters* © 2013 by Ellen Brant Voigt, by permission of W.W. Norton.

ROBERT PENN WARREN "Grackles, Goodbye," "Timeless, Twinned," and "Evening Hawk" are reprinted from *The Collected Poems of Robert Penn Warren* © 1998 by Robert Penn Warren, edited by John D. Burt, used by permission of Louisiana State University Press.

ROSANNA WARREN "A Way" appeared originally in *Poetry*. "The Line" appeared in *The New York Review of Books*.

DIANA WHITNEY "Curiosity" was the winner of the Women's National Book Association poetry prize in 2015 and originally published in The Bookwoman.

BARON WORMSER "Leaving" and "Ode to Speech" are reprinted from *Unidentified Sighing Objects* © 2016 and are used with permission of the author and Cavankerry Press.

MARTHA ZWEIG "Away/Home" from *Monkey Lightning* (Tupelo Press, 2010) first appeared in *The Marlboro Review*. "Boughbreak" from *What Kind* (Wesleyan University Press, 2003) first appeared in *The Journal*.

CPSIA information can be obtained
at www.ICGtesting.com
Printed in the USA
FFOW03n2317171017
41237FF

9 780998 260471